Alan C. Kerckhoff
Duke University

SOCIALIZATION
AND
SOCIAL CLASS

Prentice-Hall, Inc., *Englewood Cliffs, New Jersey*

FOR STEVE AND SHARI

PRENTICE-HALL SOCIOLOGY SERIES
Neil J. Smelser, Editor

Prentice-Hall International, Inc., London
Prentice-Hall of Australia, Pty. Ltd., Sydney
Prentice-Hall of Canada, Ltd., Toronto
Prentice-Hall of India Private Limited, New Delhi
Prentice-Hall of Japan, Inc., Tokyo

© 1972 by Prentice-Hall, Inc., *Englewood Cliffs, New Jersey*

ISBN: 013-819565-X

Library of Congress Catalog Card No.:
78-179620

10 9 8 7 6 5 4 3 2 1

Printed in the United States of America

CONTENTS

iii

PREFACE

The process by which an individual finds his adult place in society occurs within a pre-existent social structure. One of the features of that structure is that it is stratified, organized in levels of varying prestige. In a society such as ours, which highly values open access to all levels for all men, the fact that sons tend to occupy levels similar to those occupied by their fathers presents a problem. Does such continuity from one generation to the next constitute evidence of restricted access, or does it mean that, even within an open system, some will predictably attain higher levels than others? If the latter is the case, should the society provide mechanisms to compensate for the lack of potential so that everyone will, in fact, have equal potential for attainment?

This volume is more relevant to the first of these two questions than the second. It seeks to provide a basis for understanding how intergenerational continuity and discontinuity come about. It discusses the process of development of the individual through the pre-adult years with special reference to variations in that process that are associated with the individual's level of origin. Whether what is presented here should be viewed as evidence of restricted access, whether it calls for compensatory programs or other changes in the process, is left to the reader. The purpose of the volume is to review our knowledge of the socialization process within the context of the stratification system of the United States. Such a review is seen as a necessary prerequisite to any consideration of the value issues involved, although it is not a substitute for such a consideration.

The book covers a broad domain, and yet it is brief. My aim has been to sketch in the outlines and to provide the reader with a list of related works to which he may turn for more intensive consideration of the many topics touched on. There is thus an extensive bibliography, and numerous references to the items in it are made throughout the book. This work can to some extent, therefore, be viewed as an outline, the elements of which may be considerably expanded depending on the varied interests of the readers. I have tried to adopt a consistent perspective throughout, and to do so has sometimes meant that I had to be quite selective in my use of the available relevant materials. The reader will thus find references to other works that do not fully agree with this one, and he is urged to explore these other works in an effort to reach his own careful assessment.

I am deeply indebted to a large number of others who have dealt in depth with topics to which only limited attention can be given here. This book is an attempt to summarize and synthesize many previous efforts. As with any such work, I am also indebted to others who have assisted me. Mary Renaud prepared the Index, and Linda McDonald and Jean Brenner typed the several versions of the manuscript. I appreciate the care with which that work was done. Perhaps my greatest indebtedness, however, is to my students who asked the questions to which this volume is directed and who often suggested the answers I have found most acceptable.

Alan C. Kerckhoff

one

THE SETTING

All societies have developed specific ways of carrying out basic functions—economic production, government, family life, religion, and so on. Because of our biological life cycle, full-fledged members of any society must teach the young how to carry on the social patterns of that society if cultural continuity and social order are to be maintained.

"Socialization" is the term social scientists use to describe "the process by which individuals acquire the knowledge, skills, and dispositions that enable them to participate as more or less effective members of groups and the society" (Brim, 1966, p. 3).[1] No society leaves this process to

---

[1] As this definition suggests, the term socialization is used quite broadly. It can be used to refer to the processes by which an individual is prepared to function in *any* social unit. It is thus possible to speak of socialization for membership in a small group, such as a fraternity or an athletic team, as well as socialization for membership in the larger society. One can also study the socialization process associated with the occupation of very special positions in the society. (For instance, see Scott, 1968.) The focus of interest in this book, however, is on socialization as a general process

chance. There are always specific agencies whose task it is to prepare new members for their later activities and responsibilities. Often, different agencies carry out different parts of the process, and some coordination among them is necessary. That is to say, the process tends to be *structured,* and the new member passes through a rather orderly set of experiences that make him progressively better able to take on the responsibilities of full membership.

In every society, however, there are different *kinds* of "full members." For instance, nowhere do we find adult males and females performing the same set of tasks or being concerned with the same elements of a society's ongoing activities. Societies thus differentiate among different positions or statuses, and the incumbent of any position is expected to carry out speci-fied activities. The term "role" is used to refer to the activities that the incumbent of any given position is expected to carry out in relation to some other position in the society. Thus, an adult woman will normally have the roles of wife and mother, and possibly other roles involving economic, political, or religious activities. The adult man will also have multiple roles, and these will for the most part be different from those of his wife. Finally, to the extent that the society is "differentiated," not all adult males or adult females will carry out the same set of roles. Some will be fishermen, others blacksmiths, others religious functionaries, and so on.

Sociologists refer to society as having a "social structure," by which they mean that there are many different interrelated positions. The "struc-ture" consists of the pattern of relationships among these positions. Each position (such as father, doctor, or legislator) is related to one or more other positions (such as daughter and son, patient and nurse, constituent and lobbyist). Each of these relationships is culturally defined, thus any-one occupying a position is expected to behave in culturally defined ways toward anyone occupying any of the related positions. The set of culturally defined ways of acting toward another position is called a "role." Since any given position is likely to be related to more than one other position, there will usually be more than one role associated with a position. Merton (1957, pp. 368–84) has referred to the totality of roles associated with a position as a "role-set." And since any person occupies more than a single position (for example, he is both father and doctor), Merton refers to the totality of the positions occupied by an individual as that person's

---

preparing the individual for participation in the larger society, and the term will be used in that sense. An appreciation of both the broad usage of the term and the great array of literature relevant to the field of inquiry can be gained from an examination of such works as Goslin (1969) and Clausen (1968). Those works also show the multidisciplinary origins of the work in the field, with major contributions coming from sociology, psychology, and anthropology.

"status-set," the term "status" being used in the same way as "position" is used here.

Because of the multiple adult roles in the society, therefore, the socialization process cannot be wholly the same for all new members, and each society must provide a variety of socialization experiences. If there are many different roles in a society for which the new members are being prepared, socialization becomes highly complex. So long as the only differentiation is along such clear-cut lines as sex, it is a rather simple matter to determine which roles to prepare any individual for, and which set of socialization experiences is required. When a society becomes highly differentiated, however, so that different adult males and adult females are found carrying out a large number of rather different roles, the task becomes much more complex. A new kind of question arises. What roles should any particular male or female child be prepared to play? How is the decision made as to who receives which kind of preparation?

This book is concerned with the socialization process as it occurs in the United States, a highly differentiated society. Adult roles are quite varied, and the socialization experiences required to prepare individuals to carry them out are also quite varied. Thus, a central concern of the book will be to chart the ways in which individuals are prepared to carry out these many roles and to examine how it happens that some individuals receive one kind of preparation while others receive another kind.

It will not be possible, however, to deal with the full complexity of the role structure in the United States. We cannot hope to examine the processes by which new members are prepared to carry out *all* of the roles in society. Therefore, I have chosen to base the discussion on the fact that the United States is a society in which positions are "stratified." It is possible to view a whole cluster of positions, and their associated roles, as being similar to each other but different from other clusters. To say that our society is stratified is simply to say that some positions are viewed as superior to others in some respects. The different kinds of socialization processes that prepare people in our society to occupy such different strata or classes of positions thus become the major focus of this book.

It will be necessary to examine the basis of stratification before turning to the task of linking the classes or strata to differences in the socialization process. In fact, as the previous discussion has suggested, in order to understand the socialization process in a society, it is necessary to understand several aspects of the society's social structure. In addition to sketching an outline of our stratification system, therefore, this chapter will discuss three other structural elements of the United States. The first of these, closely related to the stratification system itself, is the fact that social mobility is both possible and highly valued in this society. That is, the American ideology rather clearly rejects the proposition that the son should necessarily take the place of his father in the stratification system. Not only should movement from one generation to the next be possible, but mechanisms to facilitate it should be made available. Another important structural feature of the society is thus the set of mechanisms used in the socialization process. Here an outline will be provided of the major agencies involved and the general stages of the process. Finally, the focal position of the nuclear family in both the stratification system and the socialization process makes it necessary to devote particular attention to our family structure.

These four features of the American social system—stratification, mobility, socialization agencies and stages, and the family—form the outlines of the setting within which socialization occurs and set the stage for the later discussion.

The socialization process may be viewed as the society's solution to the problem of continuity, the means by which members of the society develop attitudes, values, and motives, some of which may be in conflict with the conditions of life they experience. Whether the process leads to continuity or change, however, it occurs within the existent social system, and it will reflect that fact. The four features of the American social system noted here are significant conditions whose influence on the process and its outcome will be apparent throughout this volume. Although the discussion of them must be brief and must therefore ignore many complex issues, their significance cannot be overemphasized.

The Bases of Stratification

Discussions of Western industrial societies have suggested several different bases of stratification. In general, these have reflected three dimensions. Max Weber referred to these dimensions as "class, status, and party" (Gerth and Mills, 1946), whereas Lenski (1966) prefers the more descriptive terms "privilege, prestige, and power." Weber's and Lenski's terms refer to the differentiation among social positions according to their economic, honorific, and political characteristics, respectively. There is a general tendency for positions that are high or low on one dimension to be high or low on the others. That is, individuals with great wealth tend to be honored and to wield great political power, whereas poor people tend not to have high prestige and to be relatively weak politically. There are, however, many exceptions to this. The gangster may be wealthy and powerful but generally has low prestige; the religious leader may have high prestige but little wealth; and so on.

The analysis of the stratification system can, therefore, be a very complex task, and attention must often be directed to multiple indexes of position within the system. Such complexities cannot be considered here. There is considerable agreement, however, that a person's occupation is the most valid single measure of the position he occupies in the stratification system of our society. More effectively than any other single measure, occupation reflects all three of the major dimensions of stratification. In fact, this statement probably applies not only to the United States but to all modern industrial societies. As Blau and Duncan (1967, pp. 6–7) point out:

> The occupational structure in modern industrial society not only con-
> stitutes an important foundation for the main dimensions of social stratifi-
> cation but also serves as the connecting link between different institutions
> and spheres of social life, and therein lies its great significance. The
> hierarchy of prestige strata and the hierarchy of economic classes have
> their roots in the occupational structure; so does the hierarchy of political
> power and authority. . . .

In order to view occupations as the basis of classification within the stratification system, it must be possible to show that Americans actually view different occupations as superior and inferior to one another. This has been demonstrated in countless ways in sociological research. The most common point of reference used in support of the claim that occupations are differentially valued by Americans is the North-Hatt study conducted in 1947 (Reiss *et al.,* 1961). In this study, respondents were given a list of occupations and were told: "For each job mentioned, please pick out the statement that best gives *your own personal opinion* of the *general standing* that such a job has." The alternatives provided were "Excellent," "Good," "Average," "Somewhat below average," and "Poor." By assigning a score of 100 to "Excellent," 80 to "Good," 60 to "Average," 40 to "Somewhat below average," and 20 to "Poor," an average rating was computed for each occupation. The result was a distribution of occupations by prestige score like that shown in Table 1.1. Not only does this method give evidence of differential evaluation of occupations, it can also be shown that such ratings are consistently related to the income produced by the occupations and to the level of education obtained by people who hold such jobs (Duncan, 1961). Also, there is evidence that this ranking of occupations has remained very stable in the United States during the past four decades (Hodge, Siegel, and Rossi, 1964).

The ease of rating occupations and their great significance within our society have led to a concentration on occupation as an index of position in most studies of stratification. Occupation will thus provide a central point of interest in this volume. The present task is to examine the ways in which the socialization process varies by the person's location in the

TABLE 1.1
PRESTIGE SCORES OF SELECTED OCCUPATIONS*

Occupation	Score	Occupation	Score
Physician	93	Policeman	67
College professor	89	Mail-carrier	66
Banker	88	Carpenter	65
Minister	87	Plumber	63
Dentist	86	Garage mechanic	62
Lawyer	86	Machine operator in a	
Civil engineer	84	factory	60
Airline pilot	83	Barber	59
Building contractor	80	Clerk in a store	58
Public school teacher	78	Truck driver	54
Radio announcer	75	Filling station attendant	52
Newspaper columnist	74	Taxi driver	49
Electrician	73	Bartender	44
Undertaker	72	Janitor	44
Bookkeeper	68	Garbage collector	35

* Adapted from Reiss et al., 1961, pp. 54–57.

stratification system. Since the socialization process prepares the individual to take his place in the society, occupation can be viewed as an index of both the individual's origin and his later adult position. Socialization thus provides a major means by which to relate origin and destination, and both origin and destination may be meaningfully defined in terms of occupation.

Before leaving the question of the basis and measurement of stratification, one further issue must be dealt with. The discussion thus far has given little attention to education as a factor in stratification. Many students of stratification use level of educational attainment instead of or in addition to occupation as an index of social class. (See Hollingshead and Redlich, 1958). Others prefer to view education as a correlate of class position and as a means of attaining that position. (See Kahl, 1957). In the discussion that follows, education is viewed as one major part of the socialization process. It is thus seen as a means of attainment of social level rather than as a direct measure of social level. It is one of the important links between one's origin and one's destination—not only an influence in determining one's destination, but also influenced by one's origin. A major concern will be to investigate the degree to which one's educational level is a function of one's origin.

The stratification system of the United States will thus be viewed in this volume as reflected in the occupational system. It will be evident in the later discussion, however, that the investigations of relevance do not all use a single consistent index of class position. Not only are income, education, and other variables often used in addition to or instead of occupational prestige as an index of social level, but there are competing methods of indexing occupational position. Thus, it will usually be necessary to view the link between stratification and socialization from a somewhat less refined perspective than would be ideal.

In most cases, only rather crude statements will be possible, such as: "Middle class parents are more likely than working class parents to use 'conditional love' as a means of control." One would prefer to be able to make statements about the overall distribution of such techniques throughout the stratification system, but the available data are seldom adequate for that purpose. The discussion will therefore usually be limited to a consideration of differences between major segments of the class hierarchy. In most cases, the focus will be on differences between the middle class (roughly, persons with white-collar occupations) and the working class (roughly, those with blue-collar occupations). We will also examine different levels within these two major segments, most frequently the lower and higher blue-collar occupations. Here, "lower class" refers to that segment of the population whose only possible jobs are unskilled ones. Such jobs pay very little, are undependable sources of income, and thus provide a poor economic base for family stability. Families that are dependent on such jobs are thus likely to have very different lives from blue-collar families in which the wage earners have jobs that call for a degree of skill. Such skilled jobs not only are more prestigious and better paid, they are also likely to be more dependable sources of income, both because they are more essential in industry and because they tend to be unionized. The three classes to which reference will most consistently be made, then, will be the middle class, the working class, and the lower class (white-collar, skilled blue-collar, and unskilled blue-collar occupations, respectively).

Social Mobility

The fact that our society is stratified is not noteworthy; all societies show some evidence of stratification. Our society is distinctive, however, in the extent to which movement from one level to another is possible. The basic American ideology defines all people as having the *potential* for movement into other strata—higher or lower. Such movement is called "social mobility." Career mobility refers to the change of level of an individual's position during his own lifetime; intergenerational mobility refers to the difference in level of the positions occupied by a father and his son. Using occupational ratings as an index, career mobility occurs when an individual's occupation later in life has a higher or lower rating than his earlier occupation, and intergenerational mobility occurs when the son has an occupation with a different ranking from that of his father.

From the point of view taken here, both these types of mobility may involve a difference between point of origin and point of destination. For our purposes, the point of origin is defined by the individual's social level at birth, and this is determined (in our society) by his father's occupational position. If, when the individual matures, he occupies a different social level, he has been mobile. However, we may define his "destination" in terms of either his early or his later occupation. A boy whose father has a skilled blue-collar job may graduate from college, get a white-collar job, but later in life end up in a skilled blue-collar job. If we use his early occupation as our point of comparison, we would say that he has been upwardly mobile *vis-à-vis* his father—he has experienced intergenerational upward mobility. However, if we take his later job into account, he has also experienced downward career mobility, and overall he has experienced no intergenerational mobility.

A number of patterns of movement within the stratification system are thus possible, and many factors undoubtedly influence the occurrence of these patterns. To keep the discussion within manageable limits, it will be limited to a consideration of the relationship between an individual's original social level as represented by his father's occupation and his destination as represented by his early adult occupation. There will be no systematic consideration of the problem of career mobility.

There is good reason to argue that the process of socialization continues throughout one's life and does not end when one assumes the adult positions of worker, spouse, parent, citizen, and so on. The emphasis recently given in the social sciences to the processes of adult socialization is indicative of the importance of these later processes. (See Goslin, 1969, chaps. 21, 22, and 23.) The discussion here will be limited, however, to the early period of the individual's life, a period that ends when he is first called on to carry out the several adult roles. Attention will thus be limited to intergenerational mobility as defined by occupational differences between father and child when the latter is a young adult.

The presence of intergenerational social mobility in our society is, for our purposes, one of this society's crucial structural features. The fact of mobility, and the fact that everyone is not equally mobile, poses a problem. As I have said, the simple presence of stratification leads to the question of how persons are prepared to occupy different positions—how they develop the different requirements of those positions. But if there is mobility in the system, the problem is even more complex. Intergenerational discontinuity, especially if that discontinuity is selective, poses a problem.

If continuity is the norm, what brings about the discontinuous cases?

Continuity from one generation to the next is indeed found, but mobility is also common. Blau and Duncan (1967), in the most ambitious study of these issues to be made thus far, conclude that (1) continuity between father and son in general occupational level is more common than would be expected if one's origin did not affect one's destination, but that (2) there is a considerable amount of mobility in our society, and that (3) upward mobility is more common than downward mobility. Table 1.2 presents a summary of the Blau and Duncan data showing the percentages of sons from various origins whose first jobs are at various levels. All three patterns (continuity, mobility, and greater upward than downward mobility) can be seen in the table.

Blau and Duncan analyze patterns of mobility in a number of ways and conclude, among other things, that a major factor in determining these patterns is our society's increasing demand for persons at the higher occupational levels and decreased demand for those at the lower levels. More of

TABLE 1.2

MOBILITY FROM FATHER'S OCCUPATION TO SON'S FIRST OCCUPATION
FOR U.S. MALES 25 TO 64 YEARS OLD (PERCENTAGES)*

Father's Occupation	Son's First Occupation					
	Higher White Collar	Lower White Collar	Higher Manual	Mid Manual	Lower Manual	Farm
Higher white-collar (professionals, managers, proprietors)	28.6	28.2	9.8	22.6	8.5	2.4
Lower white-collar (sales and clerical	21.1	33.3	7.9	25.1	9.6	3.0
Higher manual (craftsmen and foremen)	7.4	20.5	17.4	36.0	14.0	4.6
Mid manual (operatives and service workers)	6.6	17.3	9.6	47.5	14.8	4.1
Low manual (laborers)	4.6	13.6	6.8	37.2	30.3	7.6
Farm	4.1	6.7	5.8	21.0	12.0	50.3

* The entry in each cell is the percentage of sons whose fathers were in the occupational category listed at the left whose first job was in the category listed at the top. For instance, 28.2 percent of the sons whose fathers were in higher while-collar occupations were first employed in lower white-collar occupations.

Adapted from Blau and Duncan (1967), Table J2.2.

the sons represented in Table 1.2 are in high-level occupations than were their fathers. The general pattern of upward mobility, therefore, is largely the result of changes in the occupational structure itself. There is also a general tendency for downward mobility to be restricted to movement *within* gross categories of occupations. There is little downward mobility from white-collar to blue-collar occupations, for instance, or from blue-collar to farm occupations. Blau and Duncan also find that there is generally greater *total* upward mobility (throughout one's lifetime) among those who *begin* their work lives in white-collar occupations. This latter point suggests that those with blue-collar origins who experience the most mobility make a major move from blue to white-collar positions during the period we will be discussing; the major part of such mobility is intergenerational rather than career mobility. Especially for the man with a blue-collar background, therefore, his initial job is likely to be an important determiner of his lifetime mobility. One of the central issues in later chapters will be the question of what leads some persons with blue-collar origins to make this first step into white-collar occupations and others to begin their work careers in blue-collar occupations, given the opportunity for upward mobility due to shifts in the occupational structure.

In addition to the sheer possibility of mobility within our stratification system, we must also take into account the attitudes and values associated with this possibility. Central to this set of attitudes and values is the definition of the stratification structure itself and the acceptance of the prestige hierarchy it reflects. Unless we are to view all mobility as due to random placement of individuals, we must look for factors that influence movement, and one of these factors is evidently the attraction of positions that are defined as "higher" or "better." One of the striking outcomes of studies of occupational prestige is the degree to which persons located at widely divergent points in the stratification system agree on the rank ordering of occupations (Reiss et al., 1961, Chap. 8). With only minor deviations, therefore, we may assume that there is general agreement on the relative value of occupations.

Motivation to work toward a desirable goal, however, is not simply a function of its attractiveness. It is also in large part a function of whether one believes he *can* attain the goal. It may be true that "a man's reach should exceed his grasp," but *how far* it exceeds his grasp and how clearly he sees the connection between what he can actually grasp and what he might attempt to reach are also important. Most boys learn rather early in life that the notion that "any boy can grow up to be President" is not a sufficient basis for planning one's life's work. Any boy is likely to see that some positions are so far removed from his present position that they might as well be in another world, and some positions are so foreign to his experience that he has no idea of what they are like or how he might seek to occupy them. Thus, although we will be concerned with different degrees of motivation for mobility, we will also be concerned with different views of "how the system works" and how attainable some of the generally desirable goals appear to be. These, together with the structural possibility (even necessity) of some upward mobility, constitute an important part of the context within which socialization occurs.

The Organization of the Socialization Process

The early years of life are, in all societies, a period of preparation for later activities. They are forward-looking years during which the child is told, more or less explicitly, that what he experiences is mostly preparation for adequate adulthood. Socialization is a necessary part of life in all societies. There are several ways in which the organization of this process in our society differs from that found in other societies, however, and some of these differences clearly affect the ways in which persons find their place in the American stratification system. Without attempting to provide a comparative analysis of socialization systems, I will describe some of the salient features of our own system.

Perhaps the most noteworthy feature of our socialization process, especially in comparison with socialization in non-industrial societies, is the length of time it takes. If we define the transition from childhood to adulthood in terms of participation in the labor force and getting married, it is apparent that persons in our society become adult rather late in life. This is true for men and women, and it is true whether maturity is defined in terms of marriage, working, or both. Neither marriage nor full-fledged participation in the labor force occurs for most people until after their schooling is completed. For most people, therefore, adulthood, defined in this way, is achieved only after eighteen or twenty or more years of life. Not only is this later than in most nonindustrial societies, it is also late in comparison to physical maturation, sexual maturity in particular coming well before full adult status.

The age of adulthood is not completely uniform in our society, though, and this also is an important fact for our purposes. First, we find that the age of marriage and the age of entry into the labor force vary from one social class to another. Since work and marriage are usually postponed until after the completion of one's education, people with more education tend to marry later and to become fully employed later than those with less education. The high school dropout thus tends to "grow up" in this sense earlier than the college graduate. We also find that our society is not fully consistent in its definition of maturity. For example, the ages at which one may drive a car, get drafted, buy a drink, vote, or get married without a parent's permission are not the same. It is thus quite possible for a person to be an adult by our criteria of being married and having a full-time job and still not be an adult for other purposes. This fuzziness in the demarcation between childhood as a period of preparation and adulthood as a period of full participation is thus often a source of difficulty for both the young person and for those associated with him.

A second striking feature of our socialization process is the significance of multiple socialization agencies. The family is an agency of socialization in almost all societies.[2] In highly differentiated societies such as ours, the family is only one of several significant agencies. Of agencies outside the family, the two that appear to have the greatest impact on the development of the child are the school and his age-mates ("peer group"). These two sources of influence are closely associated with each other. The fact that children go to school for a number of years, where they are separated by age levels, means that they interact much more consistently and intensively with children their own age than they do with children of other ages. The common experiences of such age-mates and the fact that they are viewed by others as "belonging together" leads to a strong sense of mutual identification. Besides being two important sources of influence, then, the school and the peer group exercise their influence largely within the same setting.

The importance of the school in our society is primarily a function of the high levels of knowledge and skill required for adequate adult functioning. Occupational demands and the requirements of everyday life necessitate a population that is both literate and analytically sophisticated. Preparation for life in this society, therefore, requires that the child be taught many skills that most parents are unable to teach him. Job specialization, and the fact that an adult in our society tends to function in a limited segment of the social system, mean that ordinarily he retains and uses only part of his education and skills.

The child, however, owing to the open nature of our stratification system, is provided with the opportunity (even necessity) of developing a broader fund of knowledge and skill that will presumably permit him to move into any one of a wide range of positions. The parent's more specialized adult experiences make him unable to provide his child with this

---

[2] One is tempted to say *all* societies instead of *almost all* societies, but there are some cases that seem to contradict such a universal statement. Perhaps the best-known is the Israeli kibbutz, in which children are reared in small groups by "nurses" or "teachers" who are not their parents. (See Spiro, 1958.) Even in that case, however, the parents do interact with their children, and most observers view the role of the parents as significant in the development of the children. Compared with the role of parents in most societies, however, the role of the parent in a kibbutz is very minor.

broader base, and the school becomes an essential agency in the process of guiding the child toward his destination in the social structure.

Peer groups assume special importance in our society because of the degree to which we expect the adult to be independent of his parents. The same emphasis on the importance of the individual that leads us to attempt to provide in the school a common basis for achievement in later life also leads us to expect that the person, as an adult, will be largely self-guided. Relations with his family of orientation (his parents and brothers and sisters), therefore, are expected to be limited as he reaches adulthood. The peer group assumes importance in the adolescent period to a large extent because of this expectation. It provides a means by which the maturing individual can assume some independence with respect to his family without divorcing himself completely from an emotionally protective environment. The limited degree to which the family can provide the child with all the necessary preparation for adulthood increases the need for other channels of exposure to the larger society. The peer group provides one such channel through which the child may be introduced to a wider set of experiences and within which he may learn some of the basic social skills not adequately taught elsewhere—group loyalty, coping with aggression, heterosexual relations, and so on.[3]

Although all three of these major socialization agencies (family, school, and peer group) have continuing contact with the young person over a number of years, each has its greatest influence at a different point in his life. In general, the impact of the family is greatest and most completely unchallenged in the pre-school years, lessening as the child gets older. The social development of the child at the age of five or six is such that the school (especially the teacher) tends to be a more significant influence than the peer group in the early school years. The most striking peer group influence is found in the preadolescent and adolescent years.

These three agencies will be the primary points of reference throughout the book, but there are other sources of socialization as well. Voluntary agencies like the Boy Scouts and Sunday schools have explicit socialization goals and attempt to influence the child's development. The mass media (television, newspapers, magazines, and movies), although not explicitly oriented toward socialization, certainly have an impact on the process. There is considerable popular concern at present about what kind of impact the media, especially television, have, but there is little reliable knowledge on the subject. Thus, although these and other sources of influence are undoubtedly worthy of consideration, it will not be possible to include a systematic discussion of them. The same is true for various special sources

---

[3] An insightful analysis of the role of age-graded groups in various societies is presented by Eisenstadt (1956).

of influence such as on-the-job training, adult education programs, and so on.

In summary, the salient features of the American socialization process are its extended length, the multiplicity of agencies, the expectation of adult independence, and the attempt to prepare children for life in a demanding society and to establish a base from which the individual can move toward any one of a number of possible adult occupational positions. The three major agencies of socialization are the family, the school, and the peer group.

The Nuclear Family

The family is an important agency of socialization, but it is also a significant element in the basic societal structure with important implications for the stratification system. Our society can best be described as having a nucleated family system. By this is meant that the small nuclear unit of husband, wife and their immature offspring form a relatively separate unit whose relations with other relatives are much more limited than are relations within the unit. It is usual for a young adult to marry and to establish a spatially, economically, and socially separate unit. Some have argued that our system is not *as* nucleated as has sometimes been claimed (Sussman and Burchinal, 1962), but it is true that relations *between* units are much more attenuated than those *within* units. Not only is the adult American expected to be an independent individual, he is expected to establish an independent nuclear family unit. The core of this family unit is the husband and wife. Children are born, are reared, and leave home to establish their own families, with the only full continuity of the unit being the parental couple.

The presence of social mobility in a society means that the child's position as an adult may be different from that of his parent. It is equally possible that the child's siblings (his brothers and sisters) may occupy a variety of different social positions and thus form units at several levels. In a real sense, it is the nuclear family *unit,* and not just the individual, that occupies a position in the stratification system. All members of the unit are classified similarly. Although the son may ultimately leave his family of orientation (his parent's unit) and establish his family of procreation (the unit in which *he* is a parent) at a different level, so long as he is defined as a member of his family of orientation, he is viewed as being a member of his parent's class. Thus, the nucleation of the family system and mobility within the stratification system are intimately related to each other. The greater the degree of an adult's independence from his family of orientation, the greater his possibility of social mobility in either direction.

When viewed in relation to the significance of occupation in the stratification system, the nucleation of the family system has other important implications. In the discussion of the bases of stratification in the United States, it was noted that an individual's occupation is the best single index of his social position. It is true, however, that this statement refers most clearly to men. The normal pattern is for young adults to marry and for the husband to be a full-time worker.[4] Even when the wife works full-time, the social position of the family is usually defined in terms of the husband's, not the wife's, occupation. Our society's general view seems to be that the wife's work activities are basically temporary and do not reflect very clearly the social standing of the family, even though they may well have significant effects on the family's economic position. With the great increase in the proportion of wives and mothers working,[5] there may be reason to expect some change in this great emphasis on the husband's occupation, but at present the emphasis is evident both in society at large and in the research activities of social scientists.

This means, of course, that the social level of the wife and of the children are dependent upon the occupation of the husband-father. It also means that the wife "marries into" and the children are "born into" a social level established by the man and that any career mobility he experiences applies to them as well, at least until the children leave home. The burden of establishing the social level of the nuclear family thus rests squarely on the man's shoulders. This responsibility has implications not only for the man's allocation of his time and energies but also for his relations with members of his family of procreation and for his socialization. Similarly, the fact that a woman marries into a social level has implications for *her* socialization. These implications will assume considerable importance in our analysis of the socialization process.

Schematic Overview

The purpose of this volume is to examine the current state of our knowl-

---

[4] Although it is common for the wife to work before the couple has children, it is much less common for her to do so when young children are in the family. In March 1967, 64.8 percent of married women under 35 years old with no children under 18 years old were in the labor force; 49.4 percent of those with children from 6 to 17 years old were in the labor force; and only 26.4 percent of those with children under 6 were in the labor force (U.S. Labor, No. 94).

[5] "In 1947, 1 out of 5 married women worked; today, 20 years later, more than 1 out of 3 is in the labor force" (U.S. Labor, No. 94, p. 10).

edge of socialization from birth to early adulthood, with particular reference to the way in which elements of the process are associated with position in the stratification system. We will study this association in two ways: first, by examining variations in the socialization experiences of persons whose *origins* are in different classes, since origin tends to determine the form and content of socialization; second, by noting the relationship that variations in socialization experiences have to social class *destination*. Since socialization is viewed as a link between one's origin and one's destination, origin will be expected to influence ultimate destination.

Yet, if socialization is *determined* by one's origin, and if one's destination is *determined* by one's socialization, then one's destination would be fully predictable from one's origin, and we know that it is not. Thus, other factors must be involved. On the other hand, the fact that there is considerable continuity in social level between generations also suggests that there is *some* relationship between social level and socialization. Although we are far from an understanding of all the factors and processes involved, an attempt is made in the following chapters to specify some of the reasons for this relationship as well as some of the reasons why it is less than perfect.

The discussion will begin with the birth of the child and follow through stages of development in which various socialization agencies and influences come into play. It will follow the child's experiences at home, in the educational system, and in the company of his peers. Throughout, there will be emphasis on variations by social level and on variations that may lead to different outcomes, whether they are related to social level or not. The discussion will take as given the stratified nature of our society, the great significance of occupation, the opportunity for mobility, the general high level of knowledge and skill required of all adults, the nucleation of the family system, the significance of nonfamilial agencies of socialization, the requirement of adult independence, and the determining significance of the husband-father's position.

Before turning to a longitudinal analysis of the socialization process within this context, however, Chapter 2 will examine at closer range some of the significant dimensions and bases of analysis that will concern us throughout. What kinds of social categories will be relevant? What aspects of social relations need to be studied? If socialization leads to the acquisition of characteristics necessary in carrying out one's later roles, what assumptions must be made about how such characteristics are acquired?

two

SOME BASIC PROCESSES

To examine the relationship between socialization and stratification, we must decide what aspects of socialization and stratification are significant. In turn, we must specify the relationship between a process (socialization) and its product (adult placement). Theoretical questions that arise include: What determines which skills, knowledge, and disposition an individual acquires? To what extent is the acquisition of any of these characteristics "clustered," so that one is likely to be found with another? Are some prerequisites to others? If the acquisition of such characteristics is related to one's origin, what aspects of one's origin are responsible for this relation? If such characteristics are related to one's destination, are they related directly (because they are needed for the person to function in that position) or indirectly (because they are necessary if one is to gain access to that position)? It would be unrealistic to claim that we are in a position to give adequate answers to all these questions. Yet, they are the kinds of questions to which this book is addressed.

To begin with, it is a basic assumption of the social sciences that such characteristics as knowledge, skills, and dispositions are learned. Although some basic biological characteristics are necessary for the learning process to occur, socialization is the process by which this potential is developed in specific directions. Without in any way questioning that individual variation in biological potential exists, or denying that such variation can influence the effectiveness of socialization experiences, the concern here will be to discuss the characteristics of the socialization process itself. In effect, this means simply assuming that the vast majority of any society's population is biologically capable of being socialized according to that society's standards, and focusing on the process by which this potential is variously directed.

But the discussion will be limited even more than this. Not only are these characteristics learned, they are learned in association with other members of society. Some significant learning occurs, of course, through experiences with the nonhuman environment, but this either is a common human kind of experience or involves other humans indirectly. For instance, although playing with toys is a meaningful socialization experience, others supply the toys and, in most cases, control the settings in which the child plays with them. It is the kinds of relations the developing person has with other people, sometimes mediated through nonhuman mechanisms, that are important here.

Given a focus on the interpersonal experiences of the individual, two basic questions are raised: (1) *Which* other people have an influence on the individual's development? Can we limit our concern to a specific other person, a small set of people, a few kinds of people? (2) In what *way(s)* do one's interpersonal experiences affect the kind of social being he becomes? What aspects of interpersonal experiences are significant in the socialization process? What kinds of influence are involved? We will consider a number of issues relevant to each of these basic questions before turning to a discussion of the chronological development of the individual.

The Significant Others

Given the nucleated family structure in the United States, the newborn child enters a very limited social world consisting of his father, mother, and possibly siblings. It is unusual for there to be anyone in the household besides a married couple and their children.[1] Typically, the child spends

---

[1] Of the 26.3 million U.S. households in which both parents lived with their children in 1960, 23.4 million had no other person present. Thus, approximately 89 percent of such households housed only a nuclear family. Of the 11 percent with others present, in the vast majority the other person was a relative. (U.S. Bureau of the Census, PC(2)4B, 1960).

a vast majority of his first few years in the company of members of that household, only occasionally encountering "outsiders" and then usually only for a limited period of time. Certainly, by any standard, the members of that small household constitute the most significant sources of human influence in the early years. Also, since the husband-father is normally the major provider for the family, and since his work activities usually occur outside the family home, the child's father spends much less time with him than does his mother. The care of children, especially infants, is viewed as a mother's obligation, and the most intense contact the young child is likely to have is with her. Such influential persons as family members are called "significant others."

As the child matures, the range of his social contacts is likely to enlarge, to include outsiders. The potential set of significant others thus increases: neighbors, relatives, friends of the parents and their children, and others may become significant others. The rate and degree of this expansion of the social world is undoubtedly quite variable, some children remaining largely within their own nuclear family units for the first five years or so, and other children experiencing a wide range of outside contacts. It is also undoubtedly true that the relationship between intrafamilial and extra-familial contacts varies. Some children, such as the child in a crowded tenement district whose only playground is the street, are able from a very early age to deal with outsiders independently. In contrast, other children seldom encounter people outside their own families except through the mediation of family members. An example is the suburban child whose mother arranges for him to play with a friend's child, and monitors the play.

Whatever the rate or extent of expansion of a child's social world in the first few years, however, all children very literally step outside the family when they go to school. The legal requirement that all children attend school establishes a second stable reference point in the enlargement of the child's social world. At this point, the set of potentially significant others is greatly expanded for every child, and school is his first big step into the larger society. At this time the teacher becomes an important source of potential influence in a way that few, if any, other adults besides his parents have been. Also, given the age-graded structure of the school, he is certain to encounter many peers.

There are thus both variation and consistency in the pattern of interpersonal contacts young children have in our society. But as the child moves out into the wider social world, through the influence of the school if in no other way, the variation in possible significant social relations increases rapidly. Although the child's family and his living arrangement may still influence the extent to which the available contacts will be made or continued, it becomes increasingly more difficult to define invariant sources of influence. This is true in part because of the large number of possible contacts, but it is even more significantly true because the maturing child becomes increasingly self-directed. As he gets older he actively *chooses* a larger proportion of his significant social contacts. However, the more invariant sources of influence (the nuclear family and the school) contribute to his development both directly, through their own influence, and indirectly, by leading him to seek other kinds of social relations. The family and school thus help to explain consistencies in choices made in the less structured situations later on.

The Influence Process

If the individual learns to be a socialized person largely through interpersonal experiences, what is there about his interpersonal experiences that influences him to develop one set of characteristics rather than another? Here the question is not so much *what* he learns but *how* he learns it. There seem to be three major kinds of learning situations involving two people, one of whom is learning something from the other. For brevity, these are referred to as *operant learning, tuition,* and *modeling.*[2]

Operant learning is the type referred to in much of classical learning theory. In the simple experimental case, the experimenter observes the subject's behavior, and when the subject behaves in the desired way, rewards him (and/or punishes him when he behaves in an undesired way). In the pure case, the only channel of influence the experimenter uses is the reward or punishment. In general, behavior that is rewarded is more likely to occur in the future, and behavior that is punished is less likely to occur.

Tuition involves a more complex relationship between the teacher and the pupil including not just overt reward and punishment but also other forms of influence, especially language. The teacher explains what is wanted, the pupil tries to perform as directed, and the teacher evaluates the performance and suggests ways of avoiding mistakes. There is a constant flow of communication between pupil and teacher, the pupil's performance of the task at hand being the subject of attention by both parties.

Modeling is an actor's use of another person as a point of reference, attempting to direct his own behavior so that it bears some specific relation to that of the other person. In the form usually cited, the actor attempts to act like the other person, but it is also possible for him to use the other as a negative point of reference and to try to act differently.

---

[2] For a more extended discussion of these three situations as they relate to socialization, see Secord and Backman (1964, Chap. 17).

There is very good reason to believe that the socialization process involves all three kinds of learning. At the same time, there are very significant differences among them that point to an essential feature of the socialization process. The relationship between the two people (the teacher and the learner) in these three forms of learning varies greatly. In pure operant learning, the teacher observes what may best be thought of as the random behavior of the learner and selects those acts that are to be rewarded. The learner need not be aware of the learning process at all. In contrast, in modeling, the learner very actively directs and limits his own behavior in accordance with his observations of the teacher's (or model's) behavior. The learner must be very much aware of his own involvement in the relationship, but the teacher may be completely unaware of the process. For example, a child may model his behavior after that of an adult who does not realize he is serving as a model. Tuition lies between these two extremes, in that tuition requires that *both* parties direct their attention to the relationship and adjust their own behavior according to the behavior of the other.

The crucial variable here, therefore, is the degree of explicit self-control of the actors. In the case of operant learning, only the teacher needs to be self-controlled; he needs to withhold sanctions until the proper time. In the case of modeling, only the learner needs to be self-controlled (at least so far as the influence process is concerned).[3] In order for learning by tuition to occur, both teacher and learner must be self-controlled. Since the newborn child is not capable of self-control, in the early part of his life only operant learning can occur. It is not until some degree of self-awareness and self-control have developed that the other forms of learning can assume importance in his development.

Self-awareness and self-control do not come about automatically, however, as part of biological maturation. In a very real sense, one must be *taught* to be aware of himself and to be able to control his own behavior. This teaching can occur only in interaction, and it is a crucial part of becoming a socialized human being. An understanding of the evolution of this human quality is necessary in order to see how such a common human process can lead to very different outcomes for people reared in different social contexts.

---

[3] In modeling, the teacher will be self-controlled to the extent he is a socialized actor, of course, and his own socialization will be a basis of the orderliness of his behavior, such orderliness making it possible for the learner to find a consistent basis for his modeling behavior.

Development of the Self[4]

language development

One frequently encounters such terms as "self-conscious," "self-control," "self-concept," and "self-image" in the literature of social science. All these terms suggest a reflexive relationship of an individual with himself. In all of them, the important feature is that the individual is an object to himself; he responds to himself in much the same way as he would to another, external object. Somehow, humans are able to "get outside themselves" in a way that permits them to take such a view of themselves. In fact, until an individual is able to do this, he is not fully able to function as a member of a social group, because he is not able to monitor his own behavior and guide it in accordance with his view of his position in the group.

It is the social setting in which humans are reared that makes such a reflexive relationship possible. The view we have of ourselves is derived from the view others have of us. The only way we can "get outside ourselves" is through the responses others make to us. By observing those responses, we learn about our own behavior, and we can in that way develop a general conception of ourselves.[5] The responses of others, however, in and of themselves, tell us only *how* these others are responding; they do not directly tell us *what* we are doing that leads to the response. Such a set of responses, if they were relatively consistent, could be a basis for the development of some kind of self-image ("I am the kind of fellow people smile at"), but it would not be an adequate basis for the development of self-control. Self-control involves not only an image of oneself as an object but the manipulation of oneself as well. To control oneself, it is critical that one know *what* is being responded to as well as the kind of response that is being made.

The key to man's refined ability to view himself as an object and to monitor and control his own behavior is language. Language consists of a set of shared verbal symbols that have come to be associated with a set of experiences. Each symbol refers to a whole set or category of experiences. It thus serves to focus one's attention on some common quality found in a set of experiences that may also have other quite variable characteristics. For instance, the word "dog" is used to refer to a highly

---

[4] The following discussion reflects the influence of the classic work of Mead (1934), Piaget (1952), and Sullivan (1953), though it is necessarily a very simplified version of their ideas.

[5] Cooley (1902) used the descriptive phrase "the looking-glass self" to refer to the importance of others' responses in the development of a conception of one's self. The phrase likens the set of significant others to a set of mirrors in which our behavior is reflected so that we can observe it—or at least its effects—more directly.

varied set of objects, whose variability is seemingly as great as or greater than their commonality. In effect, the use of the word suggests that, at least for our purposes, the common characteristics are more significant than the differences. In this way, the abstract nature of language brings some order to a set of highly variable experiences. This is one of its most essential qualities.

Two other characteristics of language are equally important for the socialization process. First, the association between the verbal symbol and the experience makes it possible to use the symbol in the absence of the experience and thereby make reference to those parts of experience that are not immediately present. Thus, we can refer to the past and in that sense reexperience it. Likewise we can anticipate the future and even discuss purely imaginary events. In this way, language enlarges the scope of our environment and experience. Second, and most important for the development of self-control, language provides an auditory experience that is substantially the same for the speaker and the listener. The speaker can monitor his own verbal behavior, and thus change his speech on the basis of what he hears himself say. It also makes it possible for him to know more precisely what he has done (said) that has led to the response of the other. Verbal behavior, therefore, is more easily monitored and more sensitively associated with social responses, than any other type of behavior.

These characteristics of language make it possible for the human being to become self-conscious and self-controlled. The newborn baby responds to the stimuli around him in much the same way as the experimental animal does. He can be, and is, conditioned, through the consistent responses of his mother, to behave in certain regularized ways. He learns that being held is associated with being fed and will make sucking movements when picked up. He learns that darkness is associated with quiet and sleep and will learn to be more active when it is light. Most importantly, he learns to associate certain sounds with some of his experiences. His mother will talk to him when feeding or changing him. When he makes certain sounds, she responds in specific ways: Crying brings her to him. Cooing leads her to respond in a nurturant way. He discovers that *he* can make sounds, and these sounds come to be associated with specific experiences. He ultimately learns that he too can make the kinds of sounds his mother makes. This learning is aided by the fact that his mother is likely to copy *his* sounds. He coos, and she coos back.[6] Given the verbal nature

---

[6] This is one limited example of a more general observation that socialization is a two-way process. Not only is the child's behavior affected by the mother, but her behavior is affected by him (see Rheingold, 1969). Since the focus here is on the preparation of children to occupy adult positions, no consistent emphasis will be given to this fact, but for other purposes, especially the analysis of adult socialization, it is exceedingly important.

of human interaction, the mother is almost certain to respond to any vocal behavior on his part, and will respond to any sound that remotely approaches a meaningful verbal symbol with warmth and affection. Thus, in a complex and repeated set of interpersonal experiences, the basic process of operant learning leads to the association between the child's vocal behavior and his mother's responses.

The child's ability to emit vocal sounds, together with the association of his own and his mother's sounds with pleasurable experiences, leads him to make such sounds even in his mother's absence. They come to have what is called "secondary reinforcement" potential. That is, the fact that they are associated with pleasurable experiences makes them rewarding by themselves. Thus, we find the baby "practicing" vocal sounds even when he is alone. As the vocal interaction between mother and child continues, she will selectively respond in a rewarding way to sounds that are (to her) meaningful, and in this way the child is encouraged to use some sounds rather than others. Eventually, the child develops the ability to make a specific desired sound in specific circumstances; he comes to associate that sound (a word, a meaningful symbol) with that situation or experience. This is the beginning of a real language, and once the general notion of the association of sounds with experiences has been learned, it is possible to build vocabulary and increase the complexity of the set of associations.[7]

It is, of course, a long journey from the mother's response to the random vocalization of the infant to his use of meaningful symbols. Once the connection between vocal acts and experience has been learned, however, it becomes possible for language to influence the learning process. A lesson that is almost certainly learned rather early by the child is that the same sound has different associations when emitted by him and when emitted by his mother. Although sounds associated with his mother's nurturant behavior come to have secondary reinforcement value to him, the rewards associated with her use of them and his are not the same. Eventually, the child comes to recognize the separateness of the symbol and the experience while at the same time recognizing the association between the two. He learns that the sound *refers to* but is not *the same as* the experience. This knowledge, together with the knowledge that the sound refers to the same

---

[7] This statement is more mechanistic and simplistic than seems justified by our knowledge of language acquisition. Some students of language (Chomsky, 1967) emphasize the learning of the logic or the "rules" of language rather than an additive acquisition of vocabulary and further complex combinations. All that is intended here is to stress the link between the mother's behavioral and linguistic responses and the child's linguistic development, whatever the specifics of that development may be. For a more extended discussion of language acquisition, see Brown (1958).

experience *no matter who emits it,* makes it possible for him to use language to "step back from" his immediate experience. Through the use of language, he can refer to the past and the future; he can relate something present to something not present; he can let others know how he is responding to a situation and can learn about their response.

A crucial part of this process is learning that objects and people, including himself, have names (identities). He learns to refer to others as "Mommy," "Daddy," "Sally," and so on, and learns that one such term applies to him. His mother refers to him by name, and he learns to do the same—"Johnny is a good boy." This is the beginning of his ability to respond to himself as an object. He learns that he is an object to others and that others respond to him as such. He also learns that they respond differently, depending on what he does. Once his language mastery is great enough, they can even tell him that their behavior toward him depends on his behavior. They label the kinds of behavior that he exhibits, and they associate their responses to him with these labels. In this way, he learns to label his own behavior in the same way—"Johnny did a bad thing."

Thus, the random vocalizations of the infant are selectively associated with a set of experiences by the mother's responses, and the gradual increase in such associations eventually leads the child to be able to refer to himself, to see himself as an object. The fact that language is abstract (thus, a single sound refers to a whole set of somewhat diverse events) provides a basis for the ordering of one's experience. The fact that language is based on vocal behavior makes it possible for the actor to experience his own behavior in much the same way as others do, and he is therefore capable of monitoring, and eventually controlling, his own behavior. And the fact that words refer to an experience but are still separable from it makes it possible to use language to separate one's thoughts from one's immediate experience. One is able to talk about, and think about, events and objects that are not immediately present. Finally, the fact that the individual is an object to others, has a name, and is responded to by means of verbal assessments, makes it possible for him to become an object to himself. Thus, he is able to respond to himself both during the course of his action and before and after he does something; he plans, monitors, and retrospectively evaluates his own behavior. In this way, he evolves a self-image, becomes self-conscious, and is capable of self-control.

This discussion of language has emphasized how the child becomes part of a verbally mediated relationship with other humans. To the extent that this development occurs, it is possible for all three learning processes to influence him. However, the simple presence and use of language does not in itself lead to the development just described, nor does it automatically make tuition and modeling effective. In effect, this section has concentrated on *what* happens but it has given less attention to *why* it happens. That issue is dealt with in the next section.

Dependency and Motivation

To understand the process by which a newborn infant evolves into a socialized adult, it is crucial to recognize the role of language in human life. It is equally important to recognize the significance of the helplessness of the human infant. Not only is it impossible for the newborn baby to survive without intensive care from adults, but the baby's dependence on others for gratification of his needs continues for a very long time. The significance of this fact cannot be emphasized too strongly. This dependence is the means through which the mature members of the child's group can influence his development. It constitutes the "hold" society has on the infant.

As noted above, one learns language basically by associating vocal sounds with the experience of need gratification. Through this process of operant learning, the mother (or other supervising adult) can control the kinds of learning that will occur. Whether or not she does it purposely, her repeated responses to the child's needs will lead him to associate her behavior with his need gratification. A number of experiences (vocal and otherwise) that are associated with (but not necessarily required for) his need gratification will thus assume secondary reinforcement value. These experiences become rewarding, in addition to those that directly gratify the infant's needs. To the extent that a single adult (the mother) is responsible for need gratification, a large number of her behavioral characteristics can be expected to assume such a reward value. The child will learn to "love" his mother in the sense that her very presence, and many of her specific actions, will be gratifying to him. Not only what she does but how she does it will be significant to him. (As a result, if another person does the "same thing" but does it in a different way, it may be much less rewarding to the child. For instance, the child who has been bottle fed by his mother for a long time may object to receiving the bottle from his father or a babysitter.) In a real sense, then, the mother *as a person* becomes rewarding to him.

This personal reward value provides the mother with an extremely powerful means of influencing him. But for her reward value (and thus her power) to be great she must respond consistently. The degree to which her behavior in response to him is viewed as "consistent" by him will depend on his being able to see a theme or a basis of orderliness in her behavior. Certainly not every act of hers will be exactly like every other act in similar circumstances.[8] As the child learns to understand verbal symbols, his mother is better able to communicate to him the basis of consistency in her responses. She can then show him how her rewards and punishments are associated with a particular principle or goal. She can define rules, definitions of good and bad, which the child can then use in directing his own behavior so as to insure rewards and avoid punishments.[9]

All this assumes, however, that the mother *has* a definition of what she wants from the child, that she can act consistently in terms of that definition, and that she can communicate that definition to the child when his verbal skills have developed sufficiently. This will not always be the case, of course. It also assumes that the child will continue to be positively motivated to receive the mother's nurturance. Certainly the early biological dependence of the child on the mother insures that he will be so motivated in infancy. Whether the mother's original hold will continue to be effective, however, will depend on how she uses it and on other sources of gratification available to the child.

Perhaps most simply put, the point here is that if the child is to *continue* to be influenced by his mother, her reward value to him must be retained as he becomes less fully biologically dependent, and he must be provided with the knowledge of how to obtain the rewards she offers. As he becomes less fully dependent biologically and as other significant persons enter his social experience (father, siblings, neighbors, and so on), the reward value of the mother potentially decreases. As the child becomes linguistically more sophisticated, and thus more analytic with respect to his experiences, he is provided with the means of gaining some conceptual distance from his social relations. The very fact that the mother is successful in providing him with the tools of language thus makes it possible for him to gain a degree of autonomy at the same time that it provides her with an additional means of influence. The balance between these two outcomes will assume considerable importance in our later discussion.

At this point, however, the important factor to emphasize is the significance of the infant's dependence on adults who attend to his needs. In our

---

[8] It is such verbal mediation of the relationship between mother and child that makes the direct applicability of operant conditioning principles to socialization so debatable. It is difficult to use any simple definition of "consistent reward" or even to define the "act" being reinforced, because a category of action rather than a single act is usually involved.

[9] As with other operant learning, however, the reinforcement value of the rewards may well be greater if they are not given with perfect consistency. Laboratory experiments demonstrate that partial reinforcement leads to the development of response patterns that are more resistant to change than those produced by means of consistent reinforcement. It is still a controversial issue, however, whether these findings are directly applicable to child socialization. (See Aronfreed, 1969.)

society, the most significant adult in this period is likely to be the mother. The way she uses the fact of the child's dependence will be a crucial factor in determining the outcome, but the intimacy of this single relationship provides the motivational force that begins the process of socialization. It makes the child attentive to the behavior of this very significant person, and it provides the means by which other socially significant learning occurs, especially the learning of language.

Values, the Self, and the Pattern of Social Relations

This chapter began with a number of questions. Two central questions had to do with (1) the specification of the significant others in the socialization of the individual and (2) the specification of the ways in which these people influence socialization. So far it has been suggested that the most significant persons in the child's life are, first, his nuclear family members (mother first, then father and siblings) and, later, his teachers, then his peers in school. It was also suggested that these significant others may influence the developing child through operant learning, tuition, and modeling. Finally, it was stated that only operant learning is an effective means of learning in infancy and that the development of language (and the associated ability to treat the self as an object) is a prerequisite for effective tuition and modeling. Motivational factors, based originally on the dependent status of the infant, are crucial, however, in all forms of learning in relation to any of these significant others.

Since the individual is viewed here as an organized entity whose learning in one situation is carried over to later situations, it is necessary not only to enumerate these several kinds and sources of influence but to consider their relationships with each other. To some extent these relationships are suggested by the ordering of the several elements in the chronology of the individual's development. Since the later discussion will show that different patterns of social relations seem to lead to different outcomes, we will consider here some of the sources of variation in these patterns.

The importance of the early association between the need gratification the infant experiences and other actions of the supervising adult, especially vocal behavior, has been stressed. This kind of association establishes the secondary reinforcement potential of these other actions and makes possible the initial stages of linguistic development. It is apparent that the degree of consistency of the behavior of the supervising adult, the frequency of such behavior, and the adequacy with which the child's needs are served will all influence the rapidity and stability of such associations. If a number of different persons provide for the infant, if the mother is inattentive to the child's needs or is inconsistent in the quality of her response, if she responds to him silently and does not reward him for emitting vocal sounds, we would not expect the development described above to occur as rapidly as it might otherwise.

If she does respond consistently and verbally, however, we would expect the child to develop linguistic skills and, within the first few years, to begin to gain the objectivity in viewing himself that has been described. The content of that self-image, however, would necessarily depend on the kind of response she and others make to him. To the extent that his mother is the most significant person in this regard, the way *she* defines his behavior will originally determine how *he* defines it. He will learn her standards of evaluation, and he will apply them to himself, just as she does. He will be most likely to do so, of course, if she continues to be a rewarding figure to him, but she must also apply standards in such a way as to threaten the flow of nurturance. Her rewards must be contingent on his behaving "properly," that is, consistent with her values. Under such conditions, he will tend to adopt her standards and attempt to direct his own behavior in accordance with them. In terms used earlier, he will tend to model himself after her.[10] Such conditions will also make learning by tuition possible. The mother's potential for reward and punishment provides the child's motivation for learning, and a shared language and the mutual adoption of standards of evaluation make it possible for both to agree on the extent to which the child's behavior is deserving of reward.

The child's adoption of standards of evaluation, together with his evolving ability to see himself as an object, provide the basis for the development of a self-conception and of self-control. The child's attention is directed to his own behavior, and he is provided with bases of differentiating among kinds of behavior. Repeated applications of the standards of evaluation (by himself and others) to his behavior make it possible for him to generalize about that behavior and about himself. He comes to view himself as one who is *generally* "good," "bad," "awkward," "clever," and so forth. The establishment of such a self-concept is an important part of his relationships with other people. He will expect others to see him as he sees himself, and he will tend to act accordingly. If he sees himself

---

[10] The literature on modeling is both extensive and filled with unresolved theoretical issues. In much of this literature the term "identification" has been used for both the process and the outcome, although even that term is used in highly variable ways (Winch, 1962). Some of the differences in theoretical position reflect different degrees of emphasis on the *behavior* that the child exhibits, as distinct from the *values* he learns. Other problems include the explanation of cases in which the child seems to adopt a *punishing* parent as a model (Cottrell, 1969); determining the degree to which maturation rather than social learning is involved; and specifying the effects of changing conditions in the child's experience upon his values and behavior. (See Maccoby, 1968, for a discussion of these and related issues.)

as awkward, he will not attempt to do things that require grace, and he will expect others to laugh if he should try.

The mother is in a highly strategic position to influence the development of a child's values and self-concept. However, even within the limited context of the nuclear family, at least one other source of potential influence will be encountered. The child's father tends generally to be less intensely involved in the everyday activities of the child, especially during infancy. He will normally interact with the child, however, and will be likely to respond in both nurturant and controlling ways. Fathers' relations with their children are evidently more variable than mothers' relations in the early years, some fathers sharing the caretaking responsibilities with the mother and others being almost wholly uninvolved. As the child matures and begins to move about the house and to use language more, however, it is almost certain that the father will become a significant figure, whatever the early relationship might have been. To the extent that the father does interact with the child, the possibility of contradictory sources of influence is introduced. If the mother and father respond differently to the same behavior of the child, if they are nurturant or punitive under different circumstances, if they apply different standards of evaluation, the child is faced with a more variable social world and will therefore have more difficulty in finding order in his experience. He will also have more difficulty in developing a consistent image of himself and adopting a set of standards by which to evaluate his own behavior.

Complete inconsistency between mother and father is highly unlikely, of course, and the reinforcement that the behavior of the two sources of influence give to each other in their areas of agreement provides a powerful incentive for the child to adopt those agreed-upon standards and accept the view of himself that such standards offer him. It would be expected, therefore, that both consistency and variety of standards and modes of response result from the presence of two significant others in the child's experience. If the child has older siblings, they will be an immediate and significant source of influence as well.

Since all individuals necessarily move from the restricted familial setting into a more diverse society, every child will come into contact with significant persons who behave somewhat differently toward him than his mother does. Becoming able to relate to such different kinds of people is, in fact, an important part of one's preparation to function in the larger society. There is undoubtedly some advantage, then, in being exposed to some diversity early in socialization, although the degree of diversity is also undoubtedly an important variable. If it is too great, the child will have difficulty developing a consistent self-image and a set of standards to guide his behavior. If there is too little diversity, the ultimate encounter with those who respond in a different way may present an overwhelming problem. Thus, some experience with diversity in the nuclear family is probably an effective way of generalizing one's view of other people so as to find a degree of unity in variable responses as well as to develop a basis of differentiation among such different responses.

The crucial factor here, however, is the degree of carryover from one relationship to another. On the assumption that others in the nuclear family respond to the child in much the same way (on the basis of many of the same principles) as the mother, the child will experience both unity and diversity. If, as he encounters others outside his nuclear family, there is some common core in the responses they make to his behavior, he will be able to abstract further uniformities from the diverse experiences. He will thereby find relatively stable principles of evaluation that will provide the basis for a relatively stable image of other people's modes of behavior.[11] This more abstract image of one's social environment and the image of the self discussed earlier are twin outcomes of the same process, the process of learning a set of self-other relationships.

To expect that a relatively consistent self-image will develop implies that there will be some consistency in the way others respond to the child, and assumes that there are general values in the society and a resulting tendency of all adults to respond similarly to similar experiences. However, it is equally true that values in our society vary and that different kinds of adults will respond differently. Men and women will tend to respond differently to aggressive behavior on the part of a child, for instance. Therefore, the child not only learns that there is some unity in a set of diverse experiences, he also learns that there is some uniformity of response from one set of persons who behave differently from another set of persons. In brief, he learns that there is social differentiation and that behavior varies according to one's social position. He thus comes to see himself as having a set of role relationships with a number of other kinds of people, and he finds that both their behavior and the behavior they expect of him differs depending on the social position these persons occupy. At first, of course, the child undoubtedly experiences this variation as variation among individuals. But he soon learns that some individuals are more similar to each other than they are to others, and when he encounters another person who has specific characteristics (for example, who is female rather than male) he expects that person to act like others he has encountered in that category. He comes to define for himself one set of expectations that are associated with one kind of person, and other sets that are associated with other kinds.

---

11 This is what many writers mean when they refer to "the generalized other." It is the image one develops of how "most other people" behave in specific circumstances. (See Mead, 1934.)

This experience of varying degrees of unity in diversity makes possible the two processes usually referred to as *role-playing* and *role-taking*. The child learns that he should behave one way with one kind of person and another way with another kind of person. These ways of behaving constitute his roles. Role-playing thus refers to the process of selecting from among several modes of interacting with others the one appropriate to a specific relationship. Role-taking, on the other hand, is the process by which the actor imagines what the other person's response would be to any one of a number of things he might do. In effect, he puts himself imaginatively in the other's place (takes his role) and decides what response to expect from the other person. On the basis of such role-taking, he can then guide his own behavior so as to elicit from the other person the kind of response he desires. Only by understanding differences among others is he able to guide his own behavior on the basis of others' expectations. Only by understanding *different* role relationships (between himself and others) can he alter his behavior so as to take the *particular* other into account. Thus, both role-playing and role-taking require an understanding of different kinds of self-other relationships, and such an understanding requires experiences with different kinds of people.

Thus, we see the maturing child as continually evolving a set of self-other concepts that he uses in guiding his interaction with other people. In new situations (such as school), he carries with him the concepts of self and others that he has already developed. Although such new situations will necessarily provide somewhat different and thus challenging relationships (a teacher, for instance, is not the same as a parent), his ability to behave as others expect him to in the new situation will depend on what has happened earlier. If he is expected to behave in the new situation much as he has been expected to behave in the past, he will have little to learn, and the transition will not be troublesome. Others in the new situation will make assumptions about him—about his definitions of right and wrong, his motives, his abilities, and so on. To the extent that he has the characteristics they assume, he will be able to perform as expected. The degree of correspondence between others' expectations and his knowledge, skills, and dispositions, therefore, will determine the degree of difficulty he experiences.

To the extent that his earlier socialization has been effective, however, he will be a self-directed actor in the new situation and will thus be less easily influenced by others should they behave in unfamiliar ways. He will not only know how his mother (for instance) expects him to behave, he will have accepted her expectations (that is, he will have "internalized" her standards and definition of their relationship). The clearer his self-image and the greater his self-control, the more likely he will be to seek to associate with others with whom he has compatible self-other expectations and the more he will attempt to avoid those with whom he has incompatible expectations. The early biological dependence becomes transformed into a preference for specific kinds of self-other relationships, those which reinforce the evolving self-image. The child learns, therefore, to seek gratifying relations with other people—people who behave as he has learned to expect them to behave. The enlarged field of possible self-other relationships, together with his role-playing and role-taking abilities, provide him with some degree of latitude in choosing which relationships to emphasize and which to deemphasize. The very process that makes it possible for him to become self-conscious and self-controlled also provides him with the basis for *evaluating* his relations with others, and his response to new social experiences will be a function of this evaluation. Both the *degree* of development of self-other expectations and the *content* of those expectations will influence his response to these new experiences.

It is possible, given this perspective, to *over*emphasize the significance of early family experiences, and some of the literature on socialization can be criticized for doing this. It should not be assumed that the child moves out of the family setting into the larger society with a fully developed self-image and a firmly established set of values. The adequacy of that self-image and the validity of the values learned through family experiences are constantly being put to the test by experiences in other settings. Just as the family controls essential sources of reward and punishment during the early years, other agencies within the society control such sanctions later on, and just as the image of self and the values adopted in the family are a function of the use of such sanctions, self-image and value commitment can change through sanctions from other sources. Thus, stability of self-image and constancy of value commitment will depend largely on the degree to which experiences outside the family are consistent with those within it.[12] The point being made here is simply that the child's response to these later experiences will be made in terms of the definitions he has already developed. To the extent that the options are open to him, he will seek experiences that reinforce those definitions, but to the extent that important sanctions outside the family are associated with different definitions, we must expect him to change.

Changes in Significant Socialization Outcomes

Thus far the discussion has focused on the kinds of interpersonal rela-

---

[12] This is the basis for Reiss's (1965) objection that studies of socialization have focused too exclusively on early experiences and on the family as the major agency of socialization.

tions that are likely to influence the socialization process, the overall dynamics of the development of self-image and self-control, and the increasingly structured and active nature of the learner's participation in the socialization process. These developments alter the nature of the social-ization process itself and make different outcomes more salient at different points in the development of the individual.

The fact that the individual's early socialization establishes character-istics that make him a more active participant in his later socialization suggests that the *kinds* of characteristics formed in the earlier period may be different from those formed later. It is not that early characteristics are not altered at a later time; moreover, characteristics whose growth is most noteworthy later on may begin to develop early. But the outcome of early socialization experiences is largely qualitatively different from the outcome of later experiences, and the outcome of the early experiences will influ-ence the later direction of development.

The discussion of socialization outcomes offered here and in the later chapters will be limited to four kinds of individual characteristics; knowl-edge, skills, values, and motives.[13] This is done both for the sake of con-ceptual simplicity and clarity and because other kinds of outcome that might be discussed can be dealt with within this four-part framework.

Certainly a child develops in all these ways in the early years. Basic skills, such as eating, elimination, walking, talking, and so on are crucial outcomes of early socialization. The child also learns a great deal of infor-mation in the pre-school years. The child's knowledge of the world, though limited in scope, is considerable. These skills and knowledge form a basis for further learning. Physical skills make the child better able to function in games with other children and to handle such important challenges as learning to write. Verbal skills are crucial in all later learning. His knowl-edge of animate and inanimate nature make it easier for him to place later lessons in a meaningful context; what he learns in school makes more sense if he already has some of the kinds of knowledge the educational system defines as important.

However, despite the unquestioned importance of the early acquisition of knowledge and skill, the acquisition of basic values and motives is a much more important outcome of the socialization process in the early years. It may be necessary to explain the basis for such a statement. The point has been made earlier that, of the three types of learning, both tuition and modeling require that the learner be self-conscious and self-controlled. It was also noted that these two kinds of learning assume greater signifi-

---

[13] In Chapter 1, Brim (1966) was quoted as saying the outcomes were "knowledge, skills and dispositions." The present statement simply further specifies two important elements of dispositions: values and motives.

cance as the child develops a self-image and becomes a more independent participant in the learning process. Both of these forms of learning necessitate that the learner be impelled toward the accomplishment of some goal(s), which may be reached more easily by participation in a relationship with a teacher or model. The learner must *want* something that he defines as *good*. In order for the learning to occur, the learner must actively participate in the process, and participation can occur only if he has developed a set of motives and values that define the relationship with the other person or its outcome—or both—as desirable. The more independent the child becomes and the more varied the sources of interpersonal influence to which he is exposed, the greater the possibility that he will choose to emphasize or deemphasize one or another relationship. The choice will be based on the degree to which the various relationships are satisfying to him, and his satisfaction will depend on his values, motives, and personal makeup.

Changes in motives and values can occur, of course, throughout life. Later chapters will be very much concerned with the influence of the peer group on them, for instance. But the very multiplicity of kinds of persons to whom the maturing individual is exposed makes it possible for him to avoid relationships that would bring about change. To this extent, it is reasonable to give special emphasis to the importance of the first few years of life in the development of the individual. A number of characteristics of socialization in these early years make it particularly resistant to change later on. The fact that some of the channeling of motives occurs at a prelinguistic level, for instance, means that motivational dynamics are not always easily dealt with at a conscious, cognitive level. The fact that basic motives and values are developed when the child is completely dependent, when characteristics of his significant other(s) assume secondary reinforcement value, means that the strength of attachment of the child to these motives and values is likely to be much greater than we might otherwise expect it to be. The strength of this attachment, together with the increasing freedom of the individual to choose to avoid relationships that threaten his motives and values and to seek those that reinforce them, is the basis for saying that the acquisition of motives and values is the most significant outcome of the early socialization experiences. Not only will such development be rather resistant to change, it will also influence the individual's definition of what kinds of knowledge and skill are significant and worth learning. Each person will evaluate the relevance of what any teacher or model has to offer in terms of his own motives and values, and he will choose to learn not only what he *can* learn (given his previously acquired knowledge and skill) but also what he *wants* to learn because it is *important*.

In contrast to early socialization, later socialization is heavily concerned with knowledge and skills, most obviously in the school setting. The "three R's" are the presumed focus of schools. The society's view of the school is as a transmitter of fundamental knowledge and skill necessary for mature functioning. It is viewed as the agency that is to provide the uniform base from which the individual may move into various adult positions. The school is presumed to be value-free in the sense that it is not to teach specific values. The controversy over prayers in the public schools reflects a degree of ambivalence about this characteristic of schools, but the official definition of value neutrality has led to the outlawing of prayers.

Thus, if we view the socialization process over the whole period of an individual's life, the most significant acquisition in the early years is a set of motives and values, whereas, by comparison, the most significant acquisition in later years is a fund of knowledge and skill. This shift in emphasis is certainly obvious as the child moves out of the home and into the school, but it is not a change that takes place suddenly. Even in school, though values are not explicitly taught, we find only a gradual shift through the grades from an emphasis on "motivating the child" to an emphasis on "learning the content," with motivation simply assumed. And, of course, even during high school and college there are other outcomes than skill and knowledge to be considered. Especially important is the influence the peer group has on the development of autonomy and the crystallization of values and motives. Yet, the major impact of the early experiences on the long-range outcome of socialization is a function of the kinds of motives and values that are established at that time. The influence of later experiences of all kinds must be seen in reference to that early development.

Summary and Forecast

This chapter has been concerned with sketching in broad outline some of the basic characteristics of the interpersonal relations and processes that are significant in the socialization process. The vast majority of children move progressively into a wider and wider set of interpersonal relations, and this expanding social context has a rather consistent pattern of growth. The most significant others, in the order of their impact on the child's development, are likely to be: mother, father and siblings, teachers and peers.

Of the three types of learning discussed (operant learning, tuition, and modeling), only operant learning can occur in the early period of the child's life. In order for tuition and modeling to occur, it is necessary for the child to be self-directed and self-controlled, and these abilities are dependent on his acquisition of language. The basic dynamic of this early socialization process is supplied by the complete dependence of the infant, which provides his mother with the means of influencing him.

The child develops self-control and a self-image in the same social context as he learns a set of motives and values. To be "self-controlled" means to be able to guide oneself in relation to some desired end. Self-control allows the child a degree of independence; he becomes an active participant in his own socialization. Since his social world is widening at this same time, he is faced with an increasingly greater choice of associations, and he is increasingly able to choose the degree of significance he will attribute to each of these associations. His choices will be a function of the values and motives he has acquired in his earlier experience. Therefore, the most significant feature of the early phase of the socialization process is the development of motives and values. By comparison, the later phases of the socialization process are more concerned with the development of knowledge and skill. However, it will be necessary throughout our analysis of socialization to see the interplay between the development of skills and the development of values. In each period the person responds to later experiences according to the results of earlier experiences, and the relationship between the earlier outcomes and this later response will need to be recognized.

Our interest in the relationship between socialization and stratification leads us to emphasize the educational system in our analysis. Education is the major societal channel of mobility, and degree of success in school is highly related to labor force participation and occupational success. The years before the child goes to school are extremely important, as the discussion in this chapter has suggested, and even during the school years the child is part of a larger network of significant social relations beyond the school. Because of the importance of the educational system in social placement, however, it will be used as the basis of organization of the discussion that follows. The discussion is organized around four periods in the child's life, which are defined in relation to his schooling, although in each period non-school experiences will be discussed as well. These four periods are the pre-school period, the elementary school years, the high school years, and the period after high school until about age 25.

The discussion of each of these periods will be concerned with: (1) the individual's position in the stratification system; (2) the structure of his interpersonal relations; (3) the degree of the individual's independence of choice; (4) the personal characteristics of the individual (knowledge, skill, values, motives); and (5) the socialization effect of the interplay between the previously developed characteristics of the individual and the nature of the current socialization experiences. A concluding chapter will return to the broad question of the pattern of relationship between socialization and stratification and will present a general model of the socialization process in a stratified society.

Throughout the discussion, some attention will be devoted to differences in the socialization experiences of girls and boys. Since married women in our society are viewed as occupying a social position defined by their husband's occupation, those characteristics and processes that lead to a woman's later position in the stratification system are likely to be different from those relevant to men. Differences in the bases for assigning position to men and women, in fact, are intimately associated with our definitions of what is appropriate male and female behavior, and girls and boys are treated differently and are expected to behave differently from a very early age. It will not be possible to consider all aspects of differential socialization by sex, but some attention will be given to differences that are associated with adult placement in the stratification system.

One socially significant social dimension will not be systematically dealt with in the body of this volume, namely, racial identity. In a society that is as aware of racial differences as this one and in which there are massive differences in the distribution of races in the stratification system, racial identity is certainly relevant to the topic at hand. An adequate treatment of that issue, however, would require a much more extended discussion than is possible here. One of the difficult issues in such a discussion would be the distinction between black-white differences that result from race as such, and those that result from the fact that nonwhites are largely found at present in the lower-class segments of the population. Throughout this book the focus is on socialization differences by social class, and those differences that are discussed here seem as relevant to the nonwhite as to the white population. This is not to say that race makes no difference but only to say that whatever differences can be attributed to race as such are *in addition to* those attributable to class. A brief appendix has been added in which some socialization differences by race are outlined.

three

THE EARLY YEARS

The first few years encompass the most impressive changes in a person's life. Anyone who observes children during the preschool years cannot help but be deeply impressed by the rapidity of their development. Within a few short years, the child changes from a wholly dependent, immobile, uncommunicative responsibility to an active participant in a complex set of relations with his physical and social surroundings. His physical development alone is a wondrous thing to behold. In a very brief period he changes from being able only to lie on his back or stomach (however he's put down) to running, jumping, hanging by his knees, throwing and catching a ball, and engaging in all kinds of intricately coordinated activities. Such activities involve a refined degree of self-control, the ability to activate and deactivate a complex set of body movements, both gross, like those involved in running, and fine, like those involved in catching a ball or drawing a picture. Although the child's physical development is hardly complete by the time he enters school, the change during the first five years is dramatic.

Equally dramatic developments occur in all functional areas. Speech is well established as part of the child's mode of interaction by the time he enters school. He is not only able to recognize but is also able to talk about many aspects of his experience—to name things, to tell about what happened at some other time or place, to ask about the reasons for events, and to verbalize his anticipations of the future. This linguistic expression is an overt manifestation of his cognitive development. His understanding of how his world is organized and how its elements function, although often incomplete and even "wrong" by adult standards, is well developed by the time he enters school. Similarly, the child's view of the world he lives in has evolved morally as well as cognitively. He sees certain acts as "good" and others as "bad," he has explanations ready for why a person might have done such things, and he expects certain outcomes from bad or good behavior. Again, these definitions, explanations, and expectations may

TABLE 3.1

TYPES OF TASKS OF EARLY CHILDHOOD SOCIALIZATION IN THE FAMILY*

Parental Aim or Activity	*Child's Task or Achievement*
1. Provision of nurturance and physical care.	Acceptance of nurturance (development of trust).
2. Training and channeling of physiological needs in toilet training, weaning, provision of solid foods, etc.	Control of the expression of biological impulses; learning acceptable channels and times of gratification.
3. Teaching and skill-training in language, perceptual skills, physical skills, self-care skills in order to facilitate care, insure safety, etc.	Learning to recognize objects and cues; language learning; learning to walk, negotiate obstacles, dress, feed self, etc.
4. Orienting the child to his immediate world of kin, neighborhood, community, and society, and to his own feelings.	Developing a cognitive map of one's social world; learning to fit behavior to situational demands.
5. Transmitting cultural and subcultural goals and values and motivating the child to accept them for his own.	Developing a sense of right and wrong; developing goals and criteria for choices, investment of effort for the common good.
6. Promoting interpersonal skills, motives, and modes of feeling and behaving in relation to others.	Learning to take the perspective of another person; responding selectively to the expectations of others.
7. Guiding, correcting, helping the child to formulate his own goals, plan his own activities.	Achieving a measure of self-regulation and criteria for evaluating own performance.

* From Clausen (1968), p. 141.

not always agree precisely with those the adults around him would give, but they influence his own behavior nonetheless.

Table 3.1 summarizes a number of these developments from the point of view of both the parent and the child. It shows the parental tasks and the kinds of achievement expected of the child. Not only the child, but the parents, have a big job in a brief period. In addition, the table makes it clear that these several tasks are interrelated. The learning of various skills requires cognitive facility; language is an essential basis of both cognitive development and value internalization; interpersonal skills presuppose knowledge of cultural values and role definitions; and so on. It is thus difficult to discuss any of these developments without discussing all of them, all at once.

What we will do here is to focus on a limited number of themes that are central to an understanding of early socialization differences at different social levels. The first question is, In what ways do child-rearing practices differ by social class? Second, how can one explain the differences in child-rearing practices? Do parents in different classes have different child-rearing goals, and is that why they use different practices? Do they have different conceptions of what practices achieve what results? Are parents in some classes less skilled than others in performing child-rearing tasks? Third, are differences in socialization outcomes associated with social level? Do children in some classes develop various skills, knowledge, values, and motives more rapidly or more fully than those in others? Are such differences in outcome related to differences in practices? In dealing with each of these questions, we have attempted to choose materials that are directly relevant to the basic question of how the socialization process acts as a link between the child's social level of origin and his social level of destination.

Child-Rearing Practices

Throughout this century, there has been an intense interest among both professionals and laymen in the kinds of influences parents have on their children. Although there have been many competing perspectives on the parent-child relationship and on what kinds of practices parents "should" use (Brim, 1959), there has been widespread agreement that what the parents do in relation to their child makes a significant difference in his development. Such interest has led to an extensive body of literature dealing with the practices used by parents and with the kinds of influence such practices can have on the child.

There has been much research dealing with children of all ages, but most has focused on the pre-school years. The reason for this concentration on the early years is partly that during this period, parents have an almost exclusive influence on the child. Theoretical considerations also enter in, however, including the strong emphasis in Freudian psychology on the psychosexual development of the child, and interest in studying parental tasks that are universal. Thus, parental practices associated with weaning, toilet training, and the channeling of aggression and sexual expression have received the most intensive investigation.

A number of studies of parental (usually maternal) behavior in relation to these socialization tasks have been carried out since the 1930s. In all these studies there was some concern with determining whether practices varied according to the social class of the families. Bronfenbrenner (1958) reviewed many of these studies in an effort to find some general pattern in the results. He concluded that although clear social class differences are discernible throughout the period covered, there have also been significant changes in parental practices. He summarizes portions of his analysis in the following way:

> Over the past quarter of a century, American mothers at all social class levels have become more flexible with respect to infant feeding and weaning. . . .
>
> Class differences in feeding, weaning, and toilet training show a clear and consistent trend. From about 1930 till the end of World War II, working-class mothers were uniformly more permissive than those of the middle-class. They were more likely to breast feed, to follow a self-demand schedule, to wean the child later both from breast and bottle, and to begin and complete both bowel and bladder training at a later age. After World War II, however, there has been a definite reversal in direction; now it is the middle-class mother who is the more permissive in each of the above areas. . . .
>
> The data on the training of the young child show middle-class mothers, especially in the postwar period, to be consistently more permissive toward the child's expressed needs and wishes. The generalization applies in such diverse areas as oral behavior, toilet accidents, dependency, sex, aggressiveness, and freedom of movement outside the home.
>
> Though more tolerant of expressed impulses and desires, the middle-class parent, throughout the period covered by this survey, has higher expectations for the child. The middle-class youngster is expected to learn to take care of himself earlier, to accept more responsibilities about the home, and—above all—to progress further in school.
>
> In matters of discipline, working-class parents are consistently more likely to employ physical punishment, while middle-class families rely more on reasoning, isolation, appeals to guilt, and other methods involving the threat of loss of love. . . .
>
> Over the entire 25-year period studied, parent-child relationships in the

middle class are consistently reported as more acceptant and equalitarian, while those in the working-class are oriented toward maintaining order and obedience.[1]

The basic difference Bronfenbrenner refers to between middle-class and working-class mothers has continued to be found since his article was written. One cannot help but wonder about the reasons for the change from before World War II to after, but the important thing for our purposes is that the class difference he describes has been consistently found since World War II. Working-class mothers tend to be more demanding of conformity and obedience from their children, even in infancy, when the demands are related to basic biological functioning.

Another aspect of Bronfenbrenner's statement should be emphasized. As one reads through these summary comments, it is striking that there is a shift from an emphasis in the early passages on what the mother *does* to an emphasis in the later passages on the overall quality of the parent-child *relationship*. This is in part a function of the fact that the studies Bronfenbrenner reviewed dealt with the entire pre-school period. As the discussion in Chapter 2 suggested, there is a change in the relationship between the mother and child during this period so far as the dynamics of socialization are concerned. Whereas operant learning is the only form of parental influence available in early infancy, both tuition and modeling become possible before the child reaches school age. Thus, it is more reasonable to focus solely on the mother's techniques during infancy than it is in early childhood. Clearly, after infancy the mother and child *inter*act, and potential maternal influence is much more pervasive than any simple operant learning perspective might suggest.

Finally, it is noteworthy that the studies referred to seldom raise the question of *why* mothers in different classes behave the way they do. When such questions are raised, it is clear that few mothers wean or toilet train their child with any view to the effect that that experience might have on the child's development. The practices seem more to reflect either traditional ways of doing things, or general views of the maturation of the infant (what he is "ready" to do), or simple matters of convenience. On the other hand, these same mothers seem to have rather clear images of what they want their young children to be and to do. As the quotation from Bronfenbrenner suggests, middle-class parents *expect* more of their children than working-class parents do.

---

[1] From *Readings in Social Psychology*, 3d ed. edited by Eleanor E. Maccoby, Theodore M. Newcomb, and Eugene L. Hartley. Copyright © 1947, 1952, 1958 by Holt, Rinehart and Winston, Inc. Reprinted by permission of Holt, Rinehart and Winston, Inc.

All of this means that any simple examination of class-related *practices* may only give us a part of a very complex picture. It is true that the age and abruptness of weaning and toilet training vary by class, and it is generally true that working-class and lower-class parents use more corporal punishment. But it is also true that such acts are only a part of the total relationship between parent and child. For instance, Kohn (1963) has argued that it may be less important to ask whether or not a parent uses corporal punishment than it is to ask *when* he uses it or any other disciplinary technique. Although the kind of sanction used may be significant, it may be much more significant to know what acts are being sanctioned. Maccoby (1961) has also argued that a narrow focus on the techniques used tends to obscure the meaning of the technique and to ignore the fact that the same technique may have very different meanings in different situations or at different points in a child's life. Such considerations as these have led to greater interest in parents' values: what they define as important, both in general and in relation to their child's behavior. It has also led to attempts to define in somewhat broader terms the quality of the parent-child relationship.

Parental Values and the Parent-Child Relationship

When one shifts his attention from the specific child-rearing techniques used by parents to the values that are being expressed in parent-child relations, it is important to view the parent-child relationship within the overall context of the life space of the family. It then becomes necessary to raise such questions as: "What values and attitudes characterize people located at different levels in the stratification system?" and "In what ways may these characteristic values and attitudes influence the parent's behavior toward his child?" Since the basic means of defining the stratification system is by reference to the occupational structure, it is helpful to examine the kinds of attitudes and values associated with different occupations.

There are three important ways in which middle-class occupations differ from working-class occupations that are relevant here (Kohn, 1963). First, middle-class (white-collar) occupations typically require the individual to handle ideas and symbols and to be skilled in personal relations, whereas working-class (blue-collar) occupations typically involve physical objects rather than symbols and call for much less interpersonal skill. Second, middle-class jobs require (or allow) much more self-direction in the ordering of activities and the selection of methods, than working-class jobs, which are more often routinized and subject to more strict supervision. Closely associated with these differences is the tendency for middle-class occupations to call for individual action whereas working-class occupations more often call for coordinated group or team action. Such occupational differences are in part the basis for requiring higher levels of education for entry into middle-class occupations. The higher the level of education, the greater the emphasis on complexity of relations in the subject matter, the greater the concern with understanding interpersonal relations, and the greater independence expected of the student.

Such differences in the occupational sphere have been shown to be associated with general value differences of adults in different social levels. Whereas middle-class people tend to value freedom and opportunity, working-class people give more emphasis to orderliness and security (Hyman, 1953).[2] The distinction in the two basic value orientations is perhaps best reflected in Kohn's (1969) terms "self-direction" and "conformity."

How does this difference in basic values affect the parent-child relationship? A quarter of a century ago Duvall (1946) argued that one could discern two different value orientations among parents that led them to behave in different ways toward their children. She called one "traditional" and the other "developmental." Traditional values, more commonly found among working-class and lower-class parents, place emphasis on order and authority. The parent is concerned that his child be clean, obedient, and respectful. The emphasis is on the child's behaving "properly," proper behavior being defined independently of any of the circumstances that may have brought about that behavior. Developmental values, in contrast, place emphasis on the child's motives and the development of self-control. This pattern, more commonly found among middle-class parents, emphasizes "internal" qualities such as consideration, curiosity, and initiative, rather than external conformity.

More recently, Kohn's (1969) research indicates that working-class parents are likely to judge the child's behavior in terms of its immediate consequences and its external qualities, whereas middle-class parents are more concerned with the child's motives and the attitudes his behavior seems to express. Kohn argues that in both cases the parent emphasizes

---

2 Others (e.g., Schneider and Lysgaard, 1953) have suggested that deferred gratification is characteristic of the middle class and that the need for immediate gratification is more common in the working and lower classes, but this is not easily demonstrated (Straus, 1962). Also, it has been emphasized in some writings (e.g., Irelan, 1966) that the very economic instability of lower-case (and to a more limited extent working-class) families discourages long-range planning, whatever the adult's values. Finally, Rodman (1963) has argued that lower-class people have a more flexible or looser value commitment than middle-class people because of the conditions they live in. Much of the literature in this area is difficult to evaluate because of methodological problems and the tendency to obscure distinctions between measures of value orientations and statements of realistic goals. Both are important, as the present discussion should make clear, but they are not the same.

in his relations with his child those qualities that are central in his own life. Middle-class life both allows and demands a high degree of self-direction, whereas working-class life places greater emphasis on authority and external conformity.

In both classes, then, parental values tend to be extensions of the modes of behavior that are functional for the parent. Middle-class parents' emphasis on self-control and initiative is tantamount to recognition of the significance of these qualities in middle-class occupations. Their emphasis on the subjective aspects of their child's development reflects the psychological sensitivity that is encouraged in both their occupations and in higher education. Their encouragement of pride in achievement, growth, and satisfaction from interpersonal relations reflects commitment to an ideal of self-fulfillment. In contrast, the working-class parents' greater emphasis on obedience and conformity reflects both their occupational experience and a lower level of faith in self-direction and initiative. Their emphasis on the external rather than the internal qualities of the child is probably in part a function of their more limited exposure to contemporary theories of the psychology of human development, but it is also due to a weaker commitment to a set of achievement values more commonly found in middle-class families. (See Rosen, Crockett, and Nunn, 1969).

This broader view of parental values, when brought together with the earlier study of child-rearing techniques, has led to the development of typologies of parent-child relations. Some of these have used the basic permissive-restrictive differentiation. Others have suggested a differentiation between love-oriented and power-assertive forms of the parent-child relationship.[3] Power assertion suggests a clear authority relationship between parent and child as well as a concern for external conformity. It is most clearly expressed in such techniques as physical punishment, shouting at the child, forceful commands, and verbal threats. A love-oriented parent-child relation, in contrast, is characterized by equalitarianism as well as a concern for the child's psychological development. It is most clearly expressed in such positive techniques as praise and reasoning, and in such negative techniques as isolation of the child and the withdrawal of parental expressions of affection.

Recently there have been suggestions that it is valuable to go one step

---

[3] Several attempts have been made to reduce the many possible dimensions of variation in the parent-child relationship to a more limited number through factor analysis or other summary techniques. Schaefer (1959) derived two basic dimensions— warmth-hostility and control-autonomy. Becker (1964) has suggested warmth-hostility, restrictiveness-permissiveness, and calm detachment versus anxious emotional involvement. Very similar dimensions have been emphasized in discussions of personality (Leary, 1957) and interpersonal relations more generally (Schultz, 1958). In the present discussion, even greater reduction of the complexity is used for the purposes of simplification and to provide a typology for later use.

beyond typologies to consider the general content of what is communicated by the parent to the child. This suggestion has taken the form of an emphasis on the significance of explanation in parental discipline. The important factor here is that the parent makes it clear to the child not only that some acts are permissible and others are not, but also *why* they are or are not permissible. It is thus important to differentiate between parental responses that are explanatory and those that are simply expressive (Kerckhoff, 1969). Although a parent's values may be inferred from his expressive responses, an explanatory response is an attempt to make those values explicit. To the extent that an explanatory response is successful in communicating the parent's values, the child has the opportunity to learn a general principle that will then permit him both to anticipate the parent's future responses and to control his own behavior in light of that anticipation. Clearly, such explanatory responses involve tuition rather than simple operant learning. To the extent that the parent also behaves according to these principles and the child comes to accept them as his own, he is also using the parent as a model.[4]

Although the evidence is only fragmentary, middle-class parents seem to be more likely than working-class or lower-class parents to use explanatory responses. This might be expected, given the middle-class parents' greater concern with the child's motives and their efforts to help him internalize a set of standards to guide his own behavior. Similarly, expressive responses and power assertion are both consistent with the emphasis on conformity commonly found in the working and lower classes. There is no perfect relationship, however, between power assertion and expressive responses on the one hand, or love-oriented and explanatory responses on the other. A parent may be quite demanding in dealing with the child, permit no deviation, and still explain in detail to the child the reason for the need for obedience and conformity. Similarly, a parent may use the withdrawal of love in response to the child's violation of parental principles without making the reason for the withdrawal clear to the child. In general, however, both power assertion and expressive responses are more common at lower social levels and love-orientation and explanatory responses are more common at the higher levels (Brody, 1968).

Explanatory and expressive responses clearly require different levels of verbal behavior by the parent. In order to be effective, an explanation must be successfully communicated to the child. The child must be led to understand the principles that underlie the parent's response. Chapter 2 emphasized the importance of language in the development of a self-image and self-control, as well as the linguistic basis of role-taking and role-playing.

---

4 The classic problem faced by the child whose parent says, "Do as I say, not as I do," is a conflict between tuition and modeling.

The parent's skill in the use of language and in teaching language to the child is evidently an important element in success in transmitting his values to the child, and the child's grasp of language is evidently an important factor in his ability to anticipate and understand the parent's (and other people's) responses. Differences in language style and mastery are therefore potentially important elements of both parental influence patterns and outcomes in the child. An examination of class-related differences in language is thus in order.

Language and Conceptual Development

Anyone familiar with *Pygmalion* (or *My Fair Lady*) knows that, at least in England, it is supposed to be possible to tell a person's social level from the way he speaks. Although the emphasis in *Pygmalion* is on the pronunciation of words, it has also been noted that people vary in the structure of the language they use. Not surprisingly, the most notable work in this area, at least for our purposes, has been done by an Englishman, Basil Bernstein. Bernstein (1964) differentiates between what he calls a "restricted" and an "elaborated" language form.

Elaborated language is concerned with logical, temporal, and spatial relationships between objects and ideas. Therefore, it has greater potential for the complex organization and analysis of experience. Restricted language use is more mundane; it is the language of subjective observation rather than analysis. The elaborated form is characterized by a larger vocabulary (especially modifiers such as adjectives and adverbs), greater use of subordinate clauses, and a generally greater grammatical accuracy and sentence complexity. These features are a means of indicating spatial, logical, and temporal relationships. Another difference is the greater egocentrism of the restricted form, egocentrism here referring to the tendency of the speaker to be less aware of or concerned with the perspective of his listener. Such egocentrism is also indicated by the use of "sympathetic circularity," a term referring to the tendency to add phrases such as "Wouldn't it?", "You see?", or "You know?" at the end of a sentence. Such phrases acknowledge the listener's existence, but they call upon him to take the view of the speaker instead of the speaker's taking the view of the listener.

Bernstein claims not only that such language forms can be differentiated but that some people rather consistently use one form to the general exclusion of the other. That is, not only are there two kinds of language, there are two kinds of language users. He also claims that the use of one of these forms rather than the other indicates the level of cognitive functioning of the speaker; the forms of speech indicate the speaker's thought processes. Finally, and most suggestive for our purposes, Bernstein claims that generally, working-class and lower-class people use the restricted speech form exclusively, whereas middle-class people much more frequently (but not exclusively) use the elaborated form.

Although the evidence is not very extensive, there are indications that these observations of Bernstein's about class differences are accurate, both in England and in the United States. In addition to Bernstein's own work, several other studies support the idea of class language differences. Lawton (1968) found greater use of adjectives and other modifiers in both the written and oral language of middle-class as compared with working-class subjects. Schatzman and Strauss (1955) analyzed the content of interviews with residents of an Arkansas town after a tornado had struck and found that the lower the social class of the subjects, the greater the egocentricity and the lower the elaboration of their statements. The middle-class speakers were more likely to take into account the perspective of the listener, whereas the lower class speakers were more apt to speak only from their own perspective. The middle-class speakers used more qualifiers and descriptive phrases to direct the listener's attention to specific aspects of the situation and to be certain he was correctly oriented before moving on with their story. Hess and Shipman (1965) call such role-taking use of language "person oriented."

Even if we assume that middle-class and working-class people do use different language forms, is there any evidence that these language forms are relevant to our concerns? Bernstein and others have argued that the use of a more elaborated language form indicates a more complex cognitive structure. Not only does such language more fully describe reality, its user can more fully analyze reality. This suggests that the egocentric quality of the restricted language indicates that the speaker does not adequately take the role of the other and thus does not adequately monitor his own speech in an effort to insure that he is fully understood. Under such circumstances, it is more likely that the speaker will not be fully understood, although it is also suggested that his more restricted cognitive structure leads him to have less complex messages to transmit.

If we attempt to apply such ideas to the parent-child relationship in the early years, we are led to expect that working-class parents would be more likely to use restricted speech forms in speaking to their children and middle-class parents would more frequently use elaborated forms. Although the message that the parent wants to communicate may be the same in both cases, the greater explicitness of the middle-class speech would lead us to expect that the latter will communicate more effectively. This, in turn, would lead us to expect that the middle-class child learns complex language earlier (McCarthy, 1954). He should also develop more complex ideas about the interaction and should become more sensitive to the need to use the same kind of elaborated speech as his parent does. Since the child's social interaction is almost wholly limited to the family in the first few years, his language acquisition will depend upon the family's verbal pattern.

There is, indeed, evidence that such class-related language differences do occur. The lower level of verbal mediation in the lower classes is suggested by a study by Spence (1967), in which he found that children from "culturally deprived" homes, though able to sort objects into homogeneous categories, were less able than other children to verbalize their rationale for doing so and less frequently could provide a name for the categories.[5] Hess and Shipman (1965) asked Negro mothers from four different status levels to instruct their four-year-old children in a simple task of sorting objects by color or type. The middle-class mothers gave explicit instructions and corrected the child's mistakes by pointing out how his action deviated from the overall instructions they had given. The mothers at lower status levels relied more on nonverbal communication (pointing and gesturing) and were seldom able to define the task clearly enough so that the child understood what he was to do. They were likely to punish or scold the child for errors, but they gave few verbal cues to explain the reason for the punishment. Not only did the middle-class children more frequently place the objects correctly, but they were also more frequently able to describe the sorting principle involved.

Finally, although using subjects who were already in school, two other studies have shown that middle-class children are more effective communicators than lower-class children. Krauss and Rotter (1968) and Cowan (1967) both presented tasks to groups of children that required one child to tell another child what to do. The second child then performed the task as he understood it. In both studies the middle-class children were better understood by *both* middle-class and lower-class children (in that the listeners more frequently performed the correct act). Moreover, middle-class children were more likely to understand the message correctly whether the teller was middle-class or lower-class. That is, the middle-class children both sent and received messages at a higher level of precision than the lower class children did. (See also Findley and McGuire, 1957; Siller, 1957).

Although the evidence is still far from complete, it does suggest that adults from different social strata do use different language forms; that

---

[5] Jensen (1968) emphasizes that both the form and the *amount* of verbal interaction varies by social class, lower-class children having less verbal experience. Lower-class children *hear* language but they get less corrective feedback about their own *use* of language (John and Goldstein, 1964).

these forms are different in their ability to communicate classificatory differences among objects in one's experience; and that the children of such adults thus tend to vary both in their own language facility and in their ability to analyze their experience according to distinct catcgorics and principles.

These language differences suggest that both the parent-child relationship and the cognitive development of the child are influenced by the language patterns used in the family. The link between language and thought is evidently an intimate one.[6] If the child has verbal labels for the categories of his experience, he is able to analyze his experience by talking to himself. He often does so audibly, as most parents have noticed (Mead, 1934; Piaget, 1952). In this way, he practices not only speech, but classification and analysis. It has been noted by those who have studied lower-class children that they are less likely than children in higher strata to whisper to themselves when they are trying to remember something (Bereiter and Engelmann, 1966). Different forms of language use, then, seem to be important for both the relationship between parent and child and the cognitive development of the child.

Hess and Shipman (1965, p. 885) summarize our current state of knowledge, especially as it applies to lower-class children, as follows:

> The picture that is beginning to emerge is that the meaning of deprivation is a deprivation of meaning—a cognitive environment in which behavior is controlled by status rules rather than by attention to the individual characteristics of a specific situation and one in which behavior is not mediated by verbal cues or by teaching that relates events to one another and the present to the future. This environment produces a child who relates to authority rather than to rationale, who, although often compliant, is not reflective in his behavior, and for whom the consequences of an act are largely considered in terms of immediate punishment or reward rather than future effects and long-range goals.

This statement suggests not only the kinds of differences in parent-child relations and the cognitive development of the child that have been dis-

---

[6] There is less than full agreement about the degree of similarity between the structure of language and the structure of thought. Sources do not agree fully as to whether one thinks only in linguistic form, whether thought without language is impossible, and therefore whether the structure of language *determines* the structure of thought. The kind of finding reported by Spence (1967) (that lower-class children could sort objects correctly but were less able to explain the principle or name the categories) is a common one, and it suggests that the child may "know" more than he can "say." It is not necessary for our purposes to state precisely the relationship between language and thought. It is only necessary to stress the intimate link between the two, a position accepted by all students of these matters. For further discussion of this issue, see Luria (1966), Vigotsky (1962), and Whorf (1956).

cussed above, but also more general outcomes in the child. With this analysis as a background, then, we raise more explicitly the question of the effects of such class-related differences.

The Social Development of the Child

Chapter 2 states that the most noteworthy socialization outcomes in the early years are related to the motivation and value commitments of the child. Such outcomes are especially significant because of the increasingly active role the child plays in his own socialization as he grows up. The motives and values that evolve during the early years provide the impetus and direction to his own later contributions to the socialization process; they define the goals he will seek and determine the strength of his strivings. Although they are not "established for all time" during these early years, the fact that the child will be a more active participant later means that he will have increasing opportunities to make choices, to seek out or ignore various kinds of experiences, to interact with or avoid different kinds of people. To some extent, therefore, he will be able to find sources of reinforcement of his previous development and to escape influences that might promote change. This avoidance will be particularly likely if many alternatives are open to him and if he defines negatively those alternatives that would lead to change.

What can be said about the development of values and motives in these early years? How is this development related to position in the status system? A full answer to such questions would go beyond the purpose of this brief volume, but it is possible to use such questions to guide our discussion of four closely related issues. The first is what has been called moral development or the development of conscience, the internalization of values. The second is the process by which achievement motivation is developed in the child. The third is the evolution of a self-image. The fourth is the growth of what will be called "social sensitivity" in the child. All four of these developments are related to factors discussed earlier in this chapter—to the structure of the parent-child relationship and to the use of language—and all four vary by social class.

Moral Development

By moral development researchers have usually meant the adoption of values by the child that lead him to define some actions as "right" and others as "wrong," and that lead him to evaluate his own behavior (or impulses) as right or wrong. Various methods have been used to determine whether or not the child has adopted such values, including projective tests, interviews, and observation. The central question from our point of view is whether some of the kinds of parental behavior described earlier are found more frequently to be associated with such moral development. The answer is clearly affirmative, although the picture is rather complex.

In Chapter 2 it was stated that the initial full dependency of the infant on his mother constitutes the basis for her potential as a socializer. To the extent that she provides nurturance, she becomes an object of the infant's love, a person whose very presence becomes gratifying. The baby's dependence makes it possible for the mother to influence him by withholding her love, by responding in a nurturant manner only when he behaves "properly." To the extent that she does this in a systematic fashion, he will learn to "prefer" to perform those acts that please her and that guarantee her nurturance and to avoid those acts that endanger or interrupt the flow of nurturance. He will come to define his acts as "good" and "bad" by adopting her standards of evaluation. Thus, of the two forms of parent-child relationship discussed earlier, a love-oriented relationship is more clearly related to the development of moral commitments than is power assertion.[7]

Power assertion tends to mediate against moral development for several reasons. First, since power assertion makes the parent the source of painful experiences, it encourages the child to withdraw from the relationship, thus reducing the parent's potential influence. Second, by providing a model of self-interest and aggression, the parent discourages the child from taking a positive view of the interests of others and focuses his attention on personal gain and threat of loss. Third, because the parent's punishment of the child's action is clearly external and carried out because of the parent's own interests, the child is encouraged to understand what those interests are, but he is not encouraged to adopt them as his own.[8]

---

[7] This statement and others that follow are based on a very extensive body of literature. Given their summary nature, they necessarily oversimplify some of the perspectives reflected in that literature. At least two refinements may be worth noting here: (1) It is important to recognize that as the child matures, he must have the opportunity to *apply* the principles that he has learned in relation to his mother. Thus, she cannot constantly monitor and externally evaluate his behavior if he is to internalize her values as his own. One aspect of the "art" of child rearing is the gradual allowance for the child's independence. (2) The outcome of such socialization experiences cannot be viewed solely in terms of the child's adoption of specific principles. Equally important is the transmission to the child of the general idea that behavior can be *principled*—guided by abstract views of right and wrong. Any full consideration of the moral development of the child must deal with both of these issues. For more extended accounts of the many complex issues involved, see Aronfreed (1969), Hoffman (1969), Kohlberg (1969b), and Maccoby (1968).

Two further points need to be emphasized regarding the relationship between a love-oriented relationship and the child's moral development. First, the use of the flow of nurturance as a means of influencing the child is effective only if the parent is basically a nurturant figure. Simply put, only a warm, affectionate parent will be able to use withdrawal of love to motivate his child to attend to and to adopt his principles of evaluation. (Sears, Maccoby, and Levin, 1957). Second, it is important that the parent not only use love-oriented techniques but also make the child aware of the reasons for the withdrawal of love. Hoffman and Saltzstein (1967) use the term "induction" to refer to the combination of love-withdrawal and explanation, especially explanation that involves the child's relationships with others. They point out that by directing the child's attention to the effect his behavior has on other people (including the parent), the child is encouraged not only to adopt the parent's principles but also to use them in directing his own behavior.

All of this suggests that there should be a set of connections from social class position to mode of child-rearing to level of moral development in the child at any given age. If parents at lower social levels more frequently use power assertion, one would expect a less well developed sense of moral commitment and understanding in children at those levels. Although the data are not fully adequate for the purpose, there is indeed evidence that this is the case. Kohlberg (1969a) has most fully assembled and synthesized the findings relevant to this issue. Although his major concern is to show that all normal children, whatever their social context, pass through the same stages of moral development, he also demonstrates some consistent differences in the rate at which this development occurs in different social classes. He describes middle-class children as moving more rapidly than working- or lower-class children from amorality to internalization and self-direction according to principles.[9]

---

[8] Psychoanalytic literature calls to our attention a process that sometimes occurs and that functions in a manner opposite to what has been described here. "Identification with the aggressor" describes the case in which a source of potential punishment is so significant and so threatening that the individual can cope with it only by adopting its principles of evaluation, even though these may violate the self-interest of the individual. Although there is evidence of such a process in extreme situations (e.g., concentration camps), and cases within family settings can be found (Cottrell, 1969), it seems unlikely that it is a frequent factor in the usual parent-child situations being discussed here. The level of surveillance, the degree of power assertion, and the seriousness of the threat to the individual's well-being is much lower in the vast majority of families than it is in such extreme situations.

[9] It is important to stress that the findings Kohlberg discusses do not suggest that lower-class children remain amoral or that they never develop moral commitments. They only suggest that this development occurs more slowly in lower social strata.

Achievement Motivation

Some of the same factors just shown to be related to moral development have been singled out as related to high need for achievement in the child. A warm, supportive mother who rewards her child with affection when he successfully performs a difficult task has been found to be associated with a high need for achievement, whereas domination and extreme control of the child, especially by the father, seem to lead to low need for achievement (Rosen and D'Andrade, 1959). Such a pattern seems to hold for boys at least, the picture for girls being less clear. If the child is to develop strong achievement motivation, he must be presented with challenges. The flow of nurturance must be controlled in accordance with the child's efforts and degree of success, but he must also be accorded sufficient autonomy to permit him to make the effort on his own. Clearly, the basic challenge is defined in terms of tasks that the *parents* see as worth performing, and their rewards tend to reinforce their own definitions of what is important. However, the general need for achievement usually dealt with in studies is not associated with specific goals. It is purported to be a more basic motivational element that can be directed toward the accomplishment of a wide range of goals. Its significance in the socialization literature is thus a function of this presumed general quality—it is as close as we have come to a general measure of goal-striving.

There is evidence that middle-class children tend to have higher levels of achievement motivation than do children at lower social levels (Rosen, 1959). Recent literature (Smith, 1968), however, has suggested that what such studies may measure is motivation to conform to externally imposed achievement standards rather than autonomous goal-setting and goal-striving. There is no adequate basis for determining the legitimacy of this suggestion, but it does help to link up the literature on achievement motivation with that on moral development. The child must not only be motivated to achieve, he must also have a set of standards by which to define what is worth achieving. An additional element also needs to be considered in this same context: the degree to which the child defines himself as one who is *capable* of achieving whatever goals are desirable. Goal-striving involves not only desire but also a view of oneself in relation to the goal that makes such striving seem reasonable. The child's self-image, therefore, is an important element in goal-striving.

Self-Image

The *clarity* of the self-image evidently depends on many of the same processes just discussed. Parents who consistently apply standards of evaluation, who communicate these clearly, and who consistently reward and punish the child according to these standards not only teach the standards to the child, they encourage him to apply those standards to himself. He thus develops a view of himself in terms of the qualities the parents emphasize. Such interaction with the parents also gives the child a view of his place in his environment. He will come to define it as friendly or threatening, as a source of opportunity or danger, as controllable or chaotic, according to how it is interpreted to him by his parents.

The *content* of the child's self-image also depends on such interaction. His sense of potency, his view of himself as potentially successful in goal-striving, begins to evolve in that interaction. How the parent sees his own relationship to the environment will affect what he tells his child, and it will thus tend to carry over to the view the child develops of himself. Here it is important to remember a point made in Chapter 1, namely, that all people tend to define the stratification system in a similar way. Thus, people at lower levels generally define *themselves* as being in low positions. They also tend to view themselves as less potent in society than do those at higher levels. This has been found to be true not only in the United States (Gurin, Veroff, and Feld, 1960), but in other nations as well (Almond and Verba, 1963). This fact helps to explain the point made earlier that lower class people tend to emphasize security more than opportunity; they have less faith that opportunity can be successfully turned to their own benefit.

Such an image of the world is the obverse side of the image of self. The person who views the world as his oyster sees not only the world but himself differently from the person who believes, "People like me don't have a chance." The self-image is thus a view of oneself in relation to one's environment. Part of that environment is the opportunity structure—how much access to rewards different kinds of people have. One's view of one's own potency, then, will in part be relative to how potent others are. This relative image is originally derived from the responses the child's parents make to his behavior and how they interpret it to the child. As he encounters other sources of evaluation and comparison, other bases of self-evaluation will also be significant. As he moves out from the nuclear family, he will come to realize not only his own level of adequacy, but also the level of adequacy and esteem of his family and of other people like him. Part of his self-image and self-evaluation will thus be based on the evaluation of *people like him*.

Therefore, both from within the family and from those outside the family, the child will gain a view of his place in his environment. Within the family, this view will be a function of the kinds of rewards and punishments he receives as well as of more specific indications from his parents regarding his potency. The parents' own self-conceptions as well as their child-rearing practices will thus both contribute to his view of himself. As he encounters others outside the family, they too will apply sanctions for his performances and they too will (both directly and indirectly) tell him how competent or potent he is.

The class-related differences in child-rearing practices can be expected to lead to different degrees of clarity of self-image for the same reasons they lead to different levels of moral development and different levels of achievement motivation. Middle-class practices provide more information and greater motivation for developing a clear self-image. The practices may also contribute to the content of the self-image. Pure power assertion, in any event, cannot provide the child with a sense of competence. In general, low self-esteem is associated with low pressure for achievement and high emphasis on compliance (Coopersmith, 1967). The particular principles used in the parental evaluations, though, are undoubtedly even more important in influencing the child's development of a self-image. The general tendency for the child to use the parent as a model and to internalize the parent's values will mean that some aspects of the parent's self-image (his view of his place in the environment) will be communicated to the child. The lower-class sense of impotence in society can be expected to influence the child in this way.

Social Sensitivity

What will be called social sensitivity is closely related to the self-image, and the evolution of social sensitivity and the evolution of the self-image occur together. By social sensitivity is simply meant the ability and the tendency to take the role of the other in social interaction. To take the role of the other, one must have some idea of what kind of response the other person is likely to make to various possible acts one might perform. Such an idea involves a view not only of the other but of one's own relation to the other. It thus necessarily requires an image of self as well as an image of the other. Such a cognitive map of self-other relations is a necessary part of both role-taking and role-playing. In general, cognitive development of children is thus closely related to their role-taking and role-playing abilities (Bowers and London, 1965; Feffer and Gourevitch, 1960). In fact it can be argued (Strauss, 1956) that learning roles (one's own and others) and learning basic social concepts are "twin processes."

The class-related practices discussed in this chapter vary in their effectiveness in encouraging cognitive development and thus role-taking and role-playing ability (Kerckhoff, 1969). The parent who effectively communicates to his child his reasons for approving and disapproving various acts not only provides his child with a more adequate basis for taking the *parent's* role, he also provides the child with a set of principles of classification that can be used in analyzing the behavior of *others* (including himself). The child thus begins to assemble the cognitive tools of role-taking in general. Finally, to the extent that the parent makes it clear that his response is based on general principles of evaluation, the dominance that is inherent in parenthood is made much less personal and arbitrary, and the child is thus better able to understand it and to approach other relationships in a more analytic way.

Summary

This section has posed the question of what consequences can be expected to flow from the different kinds of parent-child relationships discussed earlier. To the extent that these kinds of relationships are associated with levels in the stratification system, it also posed the question of how different consequences might be found at different social levels. The discussion has suggested that the kind of parent-child relationship in which the parent uses love withdrawal rather than power assertion and explanatory rather than expressive responses to the child's behavior is likely to be more effective in several significant ways. First, it is more likely to lead the child to adopt a set of standards (those of his parent) by which he can guide his own behavior. Second, it is more likely to encourage the development in the child of a high degree of achievement motivation or generalized striving in relation to standards of excellence. Third, the child's self-image is likely to be clearer and more favorable. And, fourth, the child's ability to take the role of the other (and the associated ability to guide his own behavior accordingly) is more fully developed if such a parent-child relationship exists.

In keeping with the earlier statement that the most significant kinds of developments in the early years are with respect to values and motives, the primary emphasis here has been on these developments. It should be recognized, however, that some very basic skills are an essential part of the kind of development described. Linguistic and cognitive skills, which develop together, are necessary components in the evolution of all four of the outcomes described. The motivational forces and the kinds of values internalized by the child (as well as the degree of that internalization) are the essential impelling elements in the child's later encounters with his social world. As will be apparent in the next chapter, though, not only what the child wants and how much he wants it, but how (and how clearly) he defines his position in relation to others will be significant in determining the later outcomes.

Here it has been suggested that greater moral development, a higher level of achievement motivation, a clearer and more favorable self-image, and greater role-taking and role-playing ability are associated with the kind of parent-child relationship more frequently found in middle-class families. It is important to emphasize, however, that *only as parental values and the form of the parent-child relationship vary by social class can we expect these class-related outcomes.* Since there is a less than perfect association between social class position and such elements in socialization, the patterns discussed here, though generally valid, are far from homogeneous. In fact, such imperfect relationships will be found throughout this book. It is neither possible nor consistent with the purpose of this volume to deal with all the sources of variation,[10] but it is important to remember that considerable variation occurs.

------

[10] Such variation is, of course, in part due to the fact that any division of the population into a limited number of social levels or classes necessarily places in a single category people with varied characteristics. In addition, however, there are numerous other factors, which vary within all social classes, that influence the kinds of socialization experiences a child has. From a sociologist's perspective, one of the most interesting sources of variation is the number, age, and sex of the children in the family. Birth order, spacing between the child and his older or younger siblings, and the sex of each of the children all evidently have an effect on socialization. This is a very complex and not very thoroughly investigated area of inquiry that cannot be dealt with in this volume. Relevant sources include Clausen (1966), Elder (1962), and Sutton-Smith and Rosenberg (1970).

four

ELEMENTARY EDUCATION

In the previous chapter attention was directed exclusively to the influence of the family on the socialization process. This emphasis was due to the centrality of the family in the first few years of the child's life, a centrality that results from the relative isolation of the nuclear family unit. It is an important feature of the socialization process in this society, however, that from this very restricted social setting the child moves out into an increasingly diverse and complex social environment. Although infancy in America is almost universally spent wholly within the nuclear family, children vary in the extent of their extrafamilial experiences between infancy and the time they go to school.

A number of factors influence the extent and quality of such pre-school experiences. The proximity of grandparents and other kin will affect the child's exposure to other adults besides his parents and to other significant age-mates besides his siblings. The kind of neighborhood the family lives in will be significant. The crowded tenement provides different opportunities than the sparsely populated suburb, and within either the age distribution of the residents is an important variable. Beyond the immediate neighborhood, the child may become involved in various institutions. The working mother or the parent who thinks it is "a good idea" may take her child to a nursery school, where he will spend several hours a day with adults and children in a school-like setting. Sunday school may provide a similar, though more limited experience. Finally, less formal kinds of extrafamilial experiences may be arranged by the parents, including cooperative babysitting arrangements, visits to other children's homes to play, and so on.

The significance of all such experiences for our purposes is their role in exposing the child to more diverse social relations than those within the nuclear family. Such experiences permit the child to become familiar with different kinds of people, who are likely to respond to him in somewhat varied fashion. The effect of such experiences presumably depends on the extent to which the child can discern both order and diversity in his relations with such people. These extrafamilial experiences may be viewed as either sources of reinforcement of his family experiences, sources of refinement and differentiation of his family-based conceptions of social relations, or sources of confusion and personal threat. An important factor in determining which of such effects can be anticipated will be the degree of similarity between his experiences at home and those outside. Do his playmates' parents express the same general values as his parents do in response to his behavior? Does the nursery school teacher encourage him to behave in the same way his parents do? Do his associates in nursery school or on the block act much the same as his siblings?

To the extent that there are differences between his familial and extrafamilial experiences, much will depend on the child's ability to understand and to anticipate differences in response by these others. The child may be developing the ability to do this on his own, but it is likely that he will need help in interpreting these differences. Such help may come from any of the older persons with whom he interacts, but it is most likely to come from his parents. ("Well, I guess Mrs. Jones doesn't like for you to bounce on the bed. It's all right to do it here, but you'd better not do it at Amy's house.") Thus, even when the child moves out into the wider community, the parents continue to be potentially very significant in helping him to interpret his experiences.

Whatever familial and extrafamilial experiences they have during the first five or six years of life, all children in our society must go to school. The vast majority of American children spend a large portion of their waking lives in school for at least ten years (between ages 6 and 16). Although their backgrounds may have been quite diverse, giving them quite different characteristics, the school experience provided for these children is highly uniform. This uniformity, combined with the diversity of their earlier experiences, promotes a variety of responses to the experience and thus a variety of socialization outcomes.

This chapter presents first a description of the structure of the school experience, linking it with the basic philosophy of public education and equality of opportunity in American society. Second, it considers how students coming from different backgrounds fit into this structure and how their different backgrounds influence the kinds of experience they have. A third section examines the importance of the continuing relationship between the family and the school. The role of the peer group during these early school years is then discussed, as it is related to the kinds of experiences the child has had before he comes to school and to his reactions to school. Since all of this analysis implies that children should show differences in academic performance associated with class-related variations in school experience, a fifth section discusses the evidence of such performance differences. A final section returns to an overview of the relations among socialization agencies as they influence the outcomes of socialization.

The Classroom and Equality of Opportunity

Public education is one of the most generally accepted values in American society. Although a significant minority of children attend private schools of various kinds, the great majority attend public schools, and there is little support for the idea that the education of one's children is wholly a private matter. It is uniformly believed throughout the country that the state has the right to require children to attend school, whatever their parents may think about it. Schooling is viewed as the basic mechanism by which equality of opportunity is made manifest. Even when black and white children attended separate schools, Southerners felt it necessary to claim that the schools, though separate, were equal in provision of opportunities to learn. The basic idea behind the historic 1954 Supreme Court decision (Brown vs. Board of Education) was that segregation created inherently unequal schools and that such inequality was sufficient grounds for making segregated education unlawful. As Myrdal (1944) noted many years ago, the great "American dilemma" was based on our commitment to the value of equality at the same time that we treated the Negro as inherently inferior.[1]

---

[1] This dilemma is clearly reflected more recently in the slow pace at which individual school systems have responded to the 1954 Supreme Court decision. The Appendix returns to this matter of the special place of Negroes in America.

Not only is education a functional necessity in such a technologically advanced society as ours, it is also viewed as the right of every child— a right which even his parents do not have the authority to deny him. The concern with equality of educational opportunity has led to an emphasis on uniformity. It is usual for all schools within any given system to use the same or similar materials and courses of instruction. Central supervision is thus very common, often involving statewide as well as system-wide uniformity. The significance of education to the local community, however, has also encouraged a considerable degree of decentralization. Almost no control of the individual system is permitted beyond the state level, and the tendency to impose federal standards as a condition of the use of federal funds is bitterly resisted. As a result, although there is considerable uniformity within each system, there is also considerable diversity among systems.

The school classroom reflects the basic democratic values that underlie public education (Parsons, 1959). For instance, there is a general lack of formal differentiation among children according to sex, public schools being uniformly coeducational. Similarly, no formal differentiation is permitted according to race or social status. Even where "tracking" is found, great care is taken to insure that assignment to the various tracks is not based on any other than academic grounds. This does not mean, of course, that various classes and races are equally represented in the different tracks, but only that the commitment to democratic values makes *assignment* according to class or race wholly objectionable.

The only criteria for entry to the school system are that the child be of the requisite age and that his ability fall within a very broadly defined "normal" range. *All* children within a given school district who meet these criteria are expected to go to the same school at the same time, the only exceptions being those who receive education within a parallel private system. The basic characteristics of the classroom are established by this fact. Children of the same age, from a common residential area,[2] are brought together in the classroom without regard for other qualities, and they are provided with the same educational experiences. Although the teacher is necessarily very much aware of their individual differences, and she must take them into account, she attempts to provide them with a common educational experience having a common effect. At each level, especially in primary school, there is a standard definition of "adequate performance" in such basic skills as reading and arithmetic. A fundamental goal of the teacher is to keep all her students up to the "proper level."

---

[2] This is, of course, not the case when children are "bussed" to a more distant school to accomplish some definition of racial balance. It is, in part, the deviation from the neighborhood school concept that has made bussing such a controversial practice.

In the usual case, especially in the early school years, a group of children spend practically all of their time during a given year with a single teacher.[3] This one person, usually a woman, is thus an extremely important socialization agent, providing as she does the child's initial school experience. Usually, however, the elementary school child has a given teacher for only one year. He thus has a series of teachers during his early school years while, in the usual case, many of his fellow students remain the same. The basic structure is thus one of an age-graded cohort moving from one teacher to the next at one-year intervals. This makes it possible for a given child to experience different teachers with different styles while at the same time remaining within a familiar peer context. Thus, although the teacher is an extremely important influence, the peer group provides the immediate context for that influence.

The Child and the School

Chapter 3 emphasized the importance of differences in parental values, the structure of the parent-child relationship, and family language patterns in influencing the social and cognitive development of the child. There it was suggested that such differences lead to varying degrees of value commitment, clarity of self-concept, achievement motivation, and social sensitivity in young children. Now, we will consider the significance of such variation as the children enter school. First, we will examine the significance of the varying "kinds of children" different families send to the school. This question will be examined first at a general level of analysis in which the concern will be with the kinds of child characteristics that are most congruent with the goals of the school. Then attention will be shifted to a more refined analysis in which the concern will be with the dynamics of the encounter between students and teacher.

Clausen (1968, p. 156) has described the primary aims and activities of the elementary school as:

1. Teaching and encouraging skill learning—specific cognitive skills such as reading, writing, and arithmetic, and the more general skills of maintaining attention, sitting still, participating in classroom activities.

2. Imparting information, orienting the children to the educational system and to the intellectual heritage, seeking to commit them to its ends.

---

[3] Recently, some school systems have been experimenting with "team teaching" and other nontraditional methods, but the single teacher is still the most common pattern in the lower grades.

3. Transmitting dominant cultural goals and values, making clear their meaning and relevance.

4. Providing guidance and models for problem solving; maintaining their meaning and relevance.

5. Overcoming gross deficits in preparation and attempting to deal with individual differences and with personal problems of the child that hinder his performance; in some instances consulting with the parents or with guidance personnel.

Although the school's primary emphasis is on the transmission of knowledge and the teaching of skills, it must also be concerned with values and motives. Not only must the child want to learn and accept the importance of education, he must also be able to use the proper procedures as defined by the school—such as "maintaining attention, sitting still," and "participating in classroom activities." The child's earlier development of motives, his acceptance of a given set of values, and his easy adoption of a set of procedures, therefore, will be significant factors in the ability of the school to accomplish its primary goals.

It is assumed in the educational system that the early grades must devote a considerable amount of attention to such facilitative issues—that the students must be helped to make the transition from home to school. Careful observation of children and considerable individual attention will be required so that the basic groundwork of motivation and values can be assumed in the later grades. Yet, from the beginning, the central emphasis is on *learning,* and these other matters are seen as an additional area of concern of the teacher. The school defines a "normal" level of academic performance for students at each grade level. This is true even at the point of entry; thus, it is possible for Clausen to refer to "gross deficits in preparation." It is expected, therefore, that by the end of the first year of school the students will have made measurable gains in skill and knowledge. The central goal of the teacher at each grade level is to move her charges during the year from an original performance level to one that is a year (or more) beyond that level.

Such a definition of "normal progress," together with the strong emphasis on age-grading in school, puts a premium on moving an entire cohort of students through the grades together. It also makes periodic evaluation a salient part of the school experience, evaluation that reflects the individual student's position relative both to his peers and to the external definition of proper performance at each grade level. Given the implicit assumption that the family is a potential source of assistance to the school, reports of such periodic evaluation are sent to the parents.

A student who learned in his pre-school years to want to perform well in competitive situations, who has adopted a set of values that defines education as important, who has developed self-awareness and self-control to a high level, and who already knows some of the basic knowledge and skills the school teaches is better prepared to perform according to the standards of the school. He will not be viewed as having any "gross deficits in preparation," he will be able to follow the school's procedures and his performance is likely from the beginning to be "up to standard" or perhaps beyond. The discussion in Chapter 3 indicated that the middle-class child is more likely than the child from lower social levels to have such characteristics. It thus suggests also that the middle-class child will generally enter school better prepared to participate in the educational system and to perform according to its standards.

When one examines the school situation "up close," as the participants experience it, the significance of class differences becomes even more apparent. The basic relationship in the educational process is that between teacher and student. Although most children will have had experience with adults besides their parents, for most no adult outside the family will have been so important. Unless the child has been to nursery school, the closest approximation to the relationship with his teacher will be his relationship with his mother.[4] The nature of the school situation, with one teacher and many students, makes any simple transfer of the mother-child relationship to the teacher-student relationship impossible. Nevertheless, the greater the similarity between the teacher and the mother, the easier will be the child's adjustment to the teacher-student relationship. Equally important, the greater the similarity between the child's characteristics and the teacher's expectations, the more easily the teacher will be able to guide him.

One of the most common points made in the literature on social status differences in the school experience is that the lower-class child is disadvantaged because the vast majority of teachers are middle-class in origin or at least have adopted middle-class values and modes of behavior (Carlson, 1961). To the extent that people at different status levels have different values, modes of response, and styles of speech, the lower-class

---

[4] To say this, of course, is to assume that the elementary school teacher, especially in kindergarten or first grade, is a woman. In the vast majority of cases this is true. Given the salience of the mother in the average American's pre-school experience, this probably makes the transition from home to school somewhat easier than it would be if the teacher were a man. The continued predominance of women teachers throughout the elementary, and even secondary, school years, however, is a source of serious concern for many behavioral scientists. The limited time the American father spends with his children, together with this predominance of female teachers, means that children live very largely in a woman's world. It seems likely that the clarity of sex-role differentiation is thereby reduced and that the child's development of a sexual self-image through modeling is made more difficult. Such an expectation is based on studies of the more extreme case in which the father is wholly absent (Barclay and Cusumano, 1967). In most discussions of this matter, the greater concern is with the sex-role development of boys. Given the complementary nature of the male-female relationship, however, it seems reasonable to argue that both sexes need experience with men as well as women.

child encounters in the teacher someone who is much more strange to him than she is to the middle-class child. The lower-class child has more difficulty using his previous experience as a guide in his relations with his teacher because of her different appearance, her manners, and her style of speech. Beyond this, however, it is important to remember the differences noted in the previous chapter between middle-class and lower-class parental values. The middle-class emphasis on self-control and the internalization of standards is also found in school. Middle-class teachers, like middle-class parents, look for and reward evidence of a child's commitment to middle-class values (Becker, 1952). The lower-class child's view of rules as externally imposed may not lead him to misbehave (especially in the early grades), but it is likely to lead to docile conformity to rules rather than to their adoption. He will see the teacher's expectations as very strange because of her constant emphasis on motivation and personal commitment.

The lower-class child is also less likely to have received previous assistance in learning the formal material taught by the school (Jensen, 1968; Stendler, 1951). He is less likely to know how to read or to use numbers when he enters school. Such a student will find himself lagging behind if he is with children from mixed backgrounds, but even if he is in a class-homogeneous school, he and his classmates may soon find that the teacher is unsatisfied with their performance because of her view of what constitutes normal progress. They may thus soon feel a sense of failure by the school's standards—standards they may not have fully understood or accepted in the first place.

The teacher's response to her students will reflect both her expectations of them and the institutional constraints under which she works. Her expectations will generally reflect the goals referred to earlier; she will seek to encourage the children to learn the material the school offers, through the process referred to earlier as tuition. As suggested in Chapter 2, tuition requires self-guided attention and the concern of both student and teacher. It requires the development of motives, values, self-control, and social sensitivity as discussed in Chapter 3. To the extent that her students are not ready to participate in such a process, the teacher is expected to make them ready. Given her middle-class values and definition of the adult-child relationship, she will tend to influence their development as a middle-class parent might, through love-oriented techniques and explanation (Henry, 1955).[5] To the extent that such techniques are

---

[5] Henry's analysis of such influence attempts is hardly complimentary. He sees them, where successful, as the basis of docility and the repression of creativity. The same charge has also been made against the middle-class parent for similar reasons (Green, 1946; Wylie, 1942). The point here is not to agree (or disagree) with these charges but only to emphasize the similarity between the techniques used by middle-class parents and middle-class teachers.

unfamiliar to the student, they are not likely to be very successful. The children's lack of response, together with the teacher's institutional obligation to "move on" and to at least "expose" her charges to the content of the school's curriculum, will encourage her to redefine the situation in a way that makes her position tolerable (Waller, 1932). One way to do this is to view such children as "impossible" ("not up to standard," "sweet but not very smart," "from families that work against the school," and so on). When the child is so defined, his failure to perform at the proper level and to progress to higher levels in the later grades is more "reasonable," "to be expected" (Rosenthal and Jacobson, 1968), and the teacher can better tolerate what is, by the standards of "normal progress," a failure to accomplish her goals.

The point here is not to blame the teacher (or the student) for what often happens, but only to point up the pressures they both face. From the perspective taken here, what happens is that the school does not insure the necessary base of values and motives (the degree of personal involvement) that for the middle-class child can more often be taken for granted. The institutional hold that the school has on lower-class children is weaker because the teacher has less personal influence on him. Effective tuition is less likely to occur under such conditions. Clearly, this is not a universal outcome in lower-class schools. Some teachers are much more effective than others in establishing the necessary personal tie with their students. Special qualities of individual teachers will make them attractive to particular students. Social class differences in pre-school experience, together with the dynamics of the student-teacher relationship, however, encourage the type of outcome described. This is especially so given the institutional constraints on both the teacher and the student: enforced attendance, large class size, and evaluation by uniform criteria (Bidwell, 1965; Carlson, 1964; Goslin, 1965).

The Family and the School

The child's relationship with his teacher not only builds on his pre-school experience in the family, it occurs in the context of continuing family influence. The difference in the pre-school experience of the lower-class and the middle-class child results from differences in their parents and in conditions in their homes, and these differences continue to be important after the child goes to school.

The lower-class child not only is less likely to have been taught school-related skills by his parents before going to school, he is less likely to receive help with his schoolwork later on. Lower-class parents are more likely simply to tell their children to "be good" and to punish them if they do not do well (Hess and Shipman, 1965). Lower-class children less often see their parents as interested in their schoolwork and as supportive of their efforts, and this difference by class increases as the child moves into the higher grades (Luszki and Schmuck, 1963). Teachers also recognize this difference in parental interest (Becker, 1952). The lack of lower-class parental interest is undoubtedly partly a function of the parents' own sense of impotence in relation to the school. Middle-class parents not only have a stronger educational background, which permits them to understand their children's problems and to help them with their homework, they are also more powerful in the community. The PTA is basically a middle-class organization, and middle-class parents are also more likely to attempt to influence teachers and principals as individuals than are lower-class parents.

At the same time, the increasing separation of the child from the home over long periods of time reduces the possibility of direct parental surveillance and control, and the family's hold begins to weaken. As we said in Chapter 2, love-oriented techniques of child rearing depend much less fully in the long run than power-assertive techniques on direct surveillance and control. Not only does the parent's reward potential make the child *want* parental involvement in his activities, but the child's adoption of parental values leads him to guide his own behavior more in keeping with parental wishes than would otherwise be the case. Finally, the greater the similarity between parental values and those of the school, the more consistent will be responses to the child, even outside the home.

Progress reports sent to parents implicitly assume that school and family values will be similar and that the family can help the school accomplish its goals. Reporting is done by means of the report card itself, and also through the school open house, notes from the teacher, requests for conferences, and so on. However, value similarity and effectiveness of parental assistance varies by social class. Whatever the characteristics of the students when they enter the system, the school is much more "on its own" in dealing with them if they are lower class than if they are middle class. Even with equal "inputs," therefore, the school's task would be more difficult with lower-class students, because lower-class mothers feel less confident than middle-class mothers in their relations with their children and less responsible for what the children do (Gildea, Glidewell, and Kantor, 1961).

The Role of the Peer Group

Most research on peer group patterns and their influence on the individual has dealt with adolescents, because the peer group is important in helping people make the transition from childhood to adulthood in our society. It will be necessary to consider these matters carefully in the next chapter. The limited emphasis on peer group functions in the pre-adolescent period seems to be based on the reasonable assumption that in the early grades children are not sufficiently autonomous to establish peer group norms independent of the teacher's influence. Children in the early grades tend to have one or two close friends, not many. As a result, the teacher is in a much stronger position during these years than she is later, when peer norms and values are very significant sources of influence.

It is possible, however, to err on the side of underemphasizing the significance of the peer group during elementary school. Although children enter school relatively isolated from each other and more focussed on the teacher than on each other, peer group effects are clearly seen even at an early age. Studies of nursery school children, for instance, point up the ways in which such small children reinforce each other, thereby encouraging one kind of behavior rather than another (Hartup and Charlesworth, 1967). In the early grades students display a distinct pattern of power and prestige, and bases of evaluation of self and others become apparent (Pope, 1953). Peer influences become increasingly noteworthy during the elementary school years, with greater cohesion and clearer demarcation among cliques being found in the later grades. The potency of peer influences rises during this period, reaching a peak in late childhood and early adolescence (Costanzo and Shaw, 1970). Under some circumstances group cohesion can be very strong, and membership in a group can exert intense pressure on the individual to conform to group standards (Sherif et al., 1961).

Although such peer group patterns are found with both boys and girls, they are more evident with boys. Preference for sex-specific activities and objects is found in both sexes from an early age, well before the usual time of entry into school, but such preference is much clearer with boys than with girls (Brown, 1957). Peer influences that tend to reinforce masculine forms of behavior are also apparent even from an early age (Fagot and Patterson, 1969). For both boys and girls, however, the early years in school are a period of relative isolation from members of the opposite sex. Children may withdraw from adult influence into single-sex cliques, within which the child's definition of his own sex is constantly being considered and reinforced (Maccoby, 1966). Although such a definition often takes the form of a "them-against-us" view of the opposite sex, strong expressions of distaste for the opposite sex being dominant, it has the function of emphasizing the differences between the sexes. The group provides a protective setting in which the child can develop a more coherent sex-based self-image.

Class differences in peer group relations are also apparent, and they assume even greater significance for our present purposes. Preference for sex-specific activities and items and a tendency to adopt a sex-role identity occurs earlier among lower-class children (Kagan, 1964). The potency of the peer group also seems greater among lower-class children. Lower-class children receive less direct supervision from their parents, interact with them less, and experience less support from them with regard to their school experiences. Therefore, they are influenced more by those outside the family, especially their peers (Campbell, 1964). The narrower social sphere within which such children live (they are less likely to belong to organized groups such as the church or Boy Scouts) also strengthens their ties with the peer group (Sherif et al., 1961).

The school itself tends to encourage a sense of collective identity among young children. Not only are they grouped together into a single classroom with a single teacher, they are constantly reminded of their interdependence. The scheduled events of the day involve them as a group—the several "subjects" they "do" together, recess, lunch, even going to the bathroom or getting a drink of water. Such a collective identity is, of course, highly functional from the teacher's perspective if most of the students respond positively to her attempts to influence them. The peer group and the teacher in such a situation tend to reinforce each other. This is very often what happens in the early grades, given the great significance of adults in the lives of most children.

By the same token, however, if children generally react negatively to the teacher, if she is seen as "foreign" or punitive, there is the real possibility that children will develop anti-academic values. Put the other way around, *unless* the primary school teacher uses her initial advantage from the outset to encourage the development of pro-academic motives and values, she will rapidly lose her effectiveness as a peer group structure evolves that is organized around other motives and values.

From what has been noted to this point, it seems clear that such an anti-academic pattern is most likely to develop among lower-class children, especially lower-class boys. If, as has been suggested, children from lower-class homes are generally less well prepared than middle-class children for school, if their experience in school is less consistent with their previous experience, if they receive less encouragement at home, and if their teacher disapproves of their behavior, their reactions to school and to the teacher would be expected to be less favorable. Since the school's emphasis on orderliness and receptivity are contradictory to the general cultural emphasis on physical activity for boys, lower-class boys should be especially negative about school. Given difficulties in relations with the teacher and in adhering to the performance standards of the school, and given the limited encouragement and assistance from parents, the peer group will tend to assume an increasingly significant role in the life of the lower-class boy. It provides a degree of social security and self-respect in a setting that may offer few other rewards. It presents a basis for modeling in a situation where other bases may be weak or absent, and it provides social reinforcement for successful modeling (Bandura and Walters, 1963). In fact, even at this early point in his life, the child who does adopt the values of the school and who strives for success at school may well find himself alienated from his peers (Jackson and Marsden, 1962).

The differences alluded to here are not massive when the child starts to school. Although the middle-class child is likely to begin with an advantage, and although the lower-class child is likely to experience more difficulty in adjustment and to have a sense of failure, these reactions are not uniformly found nor is there immediate evidence of grossly different responses to the school experience. It is the cumulative effects of these influences over time that is significant. The following section reviews the evidence available of the degree to which these cumulative effects are important.

Levels of Academic Performance

The discussion in the previous chapters has emphasized the importance of language in the socialization process and has referred to social class differences in language style and mastery. At school, language is both the primary medium of communication and one of the central subjects. Level of linguistic skill is a crucial basis of student evaluation. The lower-class child's more restricted language thus constitutes a problem for him, both because it is different from the language the teacher uses and because it limits his ability to perform well those tasks that are most important in school. Language differences, however, have a potentially even more destructive effect. Some have argued (Hickerson, 1966) that the middle-class teacher's constant use of a different language form and her correction of the lower-class child's language constitutes a basic attack on his sense of personal and group adequacy. If he is told that only "ignorant" people use such "poor" language, he is being asked to accept a deprecation of his family and friends, who regularly use such language. Such a basic sense of attack may not be common, but to the extent that language forms are class-related, an attempt to alter the child's language form does constitute an attempt to move him away from the standards of his family.

It is important to recognize also that it is in school that most children get their first intensive and systematic introduction to language in its written form. Compared with speech, written language is much more clearly and consistently removed from the immediate context to which it refers (Greenfield and Bruner, 1969). The child who uses a restricted language form is not as accustomed to using language in this more abstract way. In fact, as was noted in Chapter 3, even the parents of such children have difficulty talking about relationships among things without pointing to them. Written language removes all possibility of pointing or other non-verbal elements of communication. Thus, reading and writing are more of a challenge to the child who uses a restricted language form than to one who uses an elaborated form, whether or not he has had pre-school lessons from his parents.

It is not possible to consider the question of the effects of these language differences in school without taking into account another line of reasoning. Different levels of school performance by social class have most frequently been ascribed to lower-class children's being less intelligent than higher-status children. Certainly it can be shown both that measures of I.Q. vary by social class and that school performance varies by I.Q. and by social class. (See Lavin, 1965, for a review of this literature.) From the point of view of the present discussion, however, such relationships raise two questions. First, is the relationship between class and performance *only* a reflection of the relationship between I.Q. and performance? Second, given the fact that measures of I.Q. depend on the use of language, is the relationship between I.Q. and social class at least in part due to language differences between classes?

Precise answers to these questions cannot be given on the basis of current evidence, but the evidence is sufficient to suggest that social class has an independent relationship with performance (holding I.Q. constant) and that language is an important element in the relationship between class and performance. Perhaps the work of Whiteman and Deutsch (1968) is most directly relevant to these issues. In a study of first and fifth graders, they found a complex pattern of relationships among age, class, I.Q., and reading ability. Put simply, the findings suggest that: (1) even in first grade, lower-class children score lower on I.Q. tests than do higher-status children; (2) I.Q. differences by class increase between the first and fifth grades; (3) this increasing difference is greater on verbal than on nonverbal I.Q. tests; and (4) tests of reading skills show a pattern of increasing social class differences that is similar to the pattern shown by verbal I.Q. tests.[6] Thus, although I.Q. is related to social class both early and late in elementary school, the I.Q. measures themselves (especially verbal forms) seem to reflect differences in the verbal facility of children, and class-related dif-

---

[6] Whiteman and Deutsch (1968) also used an index of "deprivation" in their analysis, which is a composite index made up of very diverse factors ranging from the dilapidation of the home to the amount of family dinner conversation to whether or not the child attended kindergarten. All of these factors individually are related to social class, I.Q., and reading ability, and the composite index is related to I.Q. and reading ability, independent of social class. Also, the same study includes both white and black students, and differences by race are found, independent of differences by class. Some of these findings will be discussed in the Appendix.

ferences increase as the child passes through the primary grades. Not only does the lower-class child progressively fall farther behind in basic reading skills, such language skills appear to be reflected in the I.Q. measures themselves.[7]

Given the earlier discussion, such a progressive widening of the academic performance gap between lower- and middle-class children is not unexpected. Social class differences in the development of motives and values, differences in linguistic skills, differences in prior experience with the materials to be learned in school, and differences in the student-teacher relationship all lead to the expectation of initial performance differences. The importance of such initial student qualities in allowing students to achieve higher levels of performance also makes the progressively divergent outcomes understandable. On the other hand, to assume that such a pattern is inevitable seems unjustified. To do so involves the implicit assumption that children come to the first grade with a set of characteristics that are unchanging, and such an assumption is clearly unwarranted. Most children at all class levels seem to look forward to school and to respond to it favorably, at least at first (Stendler and Young, 1950). To the extent that the school experience is rewarding, it has the potential for significant influence. In combination with the previous and continuing family experience, and within the context of a potentially effective set of peer influences, the school can be a very influential force.[8]

In fact, the teacher's influence upon lower-class children is potentially much greater than her influence upon middle-class children. The latter generally receive assistance and encouragement at home, and they are thus better able to be academically successful *in spite of* the kind of teaching they experience. Not only is the lower-class child potentially more open

---

[7] The class differences in language may well be more complex than this discussion has suggested. For instance, Entwisle (1968) found that in some respects lower-class children were more *advanced* than middle class children when they entered first grade. Her overall findings are quite consistent with the present discussion, however, since it was in simple vocabulary measures that poor children excelled whereas the more complex and abstract linguistic forms were areas of superiority for middle-class children. She suggests that middle-class children may develop a more sophisticated view of language, which slows their vocabulary growth but increases their potential for future language development. In fact, her data show that by third grade the middle-class children were ahead of the poorer children on all measures, including those on which the poorer children had excelled in first grade.

[8] There is evidence of the importance of the teacher in the image the child has of himself in the academic setting. For instance, lower-class children are more likely than middle-class children to believe the teacher views them unfavorably, even when actual academic achievement is held constant, and the student's view of himself tends to agree with how he thinks the teacher defines him (Davidson and Lang, 1960). Such an unfavorable academic self-image will certainly influence the child's ability to function in school.

to influence by the teacher, but as we have said, the peer group is also likely to play a more important role in his response to school. Thus, *especially* in lower-class schools, the teacher needs to insure the active support of the peer group for the academic goals of the school. Moreover, all teachers, but especially the teachers of lower-class children, could profit from an understanding of group processes and the ways group norms and values evolve (Bronfenbrenner, 1970, Chap. 5).

The relevance of the peer group to level of academic performance has been clearly demonstrated by the analysis of performance levels of children in different types of classrooms (Coleman, Campbell, et al., 1966; U.S. Commission on Civil Rights, 1967). The general finding is that level of performance varies by the social class composition of the school classroom, holding ability level constant. That is, lower-class children of equal ability perform at a higher level if they are in a classroom where most of their peers are middle class rather than lower class. Not all the mechanisms by which such an outcome occurs are fully understood, but is seems clear that the peer group is an important influence on a child's school performance.

Such influence probably also varies by the sex of the child. Even in the early grades, girls tend to out-perform boys (Hughes, 1953). It may be (Parsons, 1949) that their higher performance is due to the fact that the classroom tends to be dominated by female values, in part because the teacher is usually female. The more active behavior patterns of boys may lead them to violate the teacher's expectations more often, and her negative response may encourage more powerful anti-academic values to develop among boys. It might also be that such performance differences are actually due to teachers' preference for girls' qualities, a preference that leads them to work harder with girls as a result.

Whatever the reason for the sex-linked difference in performance, it is certainly of great social significance if boys are even more likely than girls to be subject to anti-academic peer influences. Given the central position of work in the adult life of men in our society, and given the importance of education as a channel to occupational attainment, it would be particularly dysfunctional if boys were "turned off" by the early school experience. It may well be, in fact, that the societal emphasis on the active, manipulative features of the male role contributes to the boys' sense of alienation from school. Boys learn very early that "being a man" involves accomplishing tangible goals in the environment. If the school's goals are seen as wholly internal (self-development, learning for its own sake), their relevance to being a man may not be obvious. In contrast, peer standards, which almost certainly will involve physical activity and the challenge of overt accomplishments, are likely to be much more attractive. In short, it may be necessary to provide a more active kind of school experience for boys in which tangible goals are provided that arc clcarly rclevant to the evolution of a masculine self-image. This would be particularly true in the lower class, where "being a man" more often involves physical activity. A female teacher may well be able to provide such experiences, but some alteration in the usual orderly, cognitively oriented classroom pattern would presumably be required.

Multiple Socialization Agencies and the Opportunity Structure

One of the characteristics of the socialization process in the United States that was stressed in Chapter 1 was the presence of multiple agencies of socialization. It was noted in that discussion that the high level of knowledge and skill required for normal adult functioning in our society, together with the separation of the home and the work place and the nucleation of the family system, make separate educational institutions more functional than they might be in another kind of social system. The family, which is a major agency of socialization in the vast majority of societies, cannot provide all the socialization experiences the American child needs to become a functioning adult. The family and the school both make contributions to the child's socialization, and normally these are complementary. The family normally provides the child with a sense of identity, a set of values, and the motivational base for his later actions, while the school provides him with the knowledge and skills necessary to accomplish the goals he seeks. To see the contributions of these two agencies as purely additive, however, would be an oversimplification, because family and school interact. To sum up what we have said before, the values and motives the child acquires within the family provide a basis for his response to the school program. The degree to which he *wants* and sees the *importance* of what the school has to offer depends largely on what he has learned in the family. Also, the degree to which he *can* learn what the school has to offer depends largely on what cognitive and linguistic skills he has developed before going to school as well as the amount and kind of assistance he receives at home during his early school years. The child's response to the school is thus very clearly influenced by his experience in the family.

The opposite is also true, however. Although values and motives are a major contribution of the family in the socialization process, *any* significant social experience is capable of influencing the child's values and motives. The child's relationship with the teacher can be a very intense one, and her influence on what he values and how hard he strives for his goals can be highly significant. The emphasis of the primary school on motivating the child to want to do well within the academic setting leads to the teacher's attempts to provide him with a rewarding experience. To the extent she is successful, he will adopt her (actually, the school's) values and standards of evaluation. He will want to do well in school. The implicit assumption in most schools is that much of this motivational and value base has been established before the child gets to school, and it is only necessary for the teacher to build upon it. If that is not true, however, the child may not learn to value school performance, and the cumulative deficit discussed above is more likely to occur. It is equally true, though, that the successful teacher may provide the child with a set of motives and values he had not acquired in the family. In some cases, this may be somewhat in the nature of "filling a vacuum." In the extreme case, however, what he learns to value in school may come in conflict with what he is taught to value at home, and the school may actually "wean him away from" the standards of his family.

The earlier discussion also stressed a third socialization agency, the peer group. The effect of the peer group is especially significant because of the structural characteristics of the family and the school. In the family, the child has only limited experience with people his own age, whereas in school this is a major part of his experience. Relations with peers are, by definition, relations among equals, and they are thus more open than relations with elders, unstructured, and subject to the influence of the personal qualities of the individuals. Peer groups, however, are organized around values and norms that are used to judge not only members of the group itself but also their relations with "outsiders." It has been suggested previously that the teacher is, at least to some degree, an "outsider." Given the unorganized nature of peer relations in the first grade, she may have an opportunity to influence the development of peer values and norms so that they become organized around the values and norms of the school. If she is successful in this, the social power of the peer group can help her accomplish her educational goals. If the students see the teacher as a stranger, however, as one who is not only different but even threatening, that same social power can operate to subvert her educational goals.

There is a similar relationship between the peer group and the family. If the school serves a homogeneous neighborhood, family standards will be similar. Assuming a continuing effective influence from their families, the peer and family influences may be highly reinforcing, at least in the early school years. The child who attends a school in which most of his peers have different values from those he has experienced in the family, however, will be subject to peer group pressures that will contradict his parents' influence. In a highly mixed school setting, students may divide into several competitive or even combative peer groups that may provide an even more complex set of potential sources of influence for some children.[9]

The three-way relationship among the family, the school, and the peer group thus constitutes a social matrix within which the child has potentially diverse socialization experiences. In some cases (for example, a middle class suburban setting), all three socialization agencies may tend to reinforce each other, but usually, varying degrees of inconsistency will be experienced. The poor black child who goes to a predominantly white lower-class school with a middle-class teacher (white or black) will not have a consistent experience. The "lessons" he learns from his peers, his teachers, and his family will not be the same. In such a situation, it is difficult to predict the outcome with confidence. It seems unlikely, however, that the school can successfully transmit to the child the knowledge and skill that is its major unique contribution to the socialization process if both the family and the peer group standards are antithetical or unsupportive. Unless the school can enlist the active support of at least one of these other important socialization agencies, only the most exceptional teacher can accomplish the goals of the school.

Given this three-way relationship among family, school, and peer group, it is not surprising that there is less than complete continuity between parent and child in social and personal characteristics. The extrafamilial influences are potentially extremely strong, and they can affect the child's values and motives as well as his knowledge and skills. What a person values as an adult, therefore, may be rather different from what his parents valued when he was a child. He may become a very different kind of person from his parents. Such extrafamilial influences also affect his social position as an adult. Success in school is an important prerequisite to entrance to most higher occupations, and the basis of academic success is being established from the early grades onward. An early rejection of academic standards is likely to be the first step toward academic failure and low social position later on.

It is equally important, however, to keep another aspect of the child's experience in mind, namely, the opportunities open to him. Access to good schools with talented, highly motivated teachers is one of the first instances of the importance of opportunity. For the child from a family in which academic values are not stressed and in which assistance and encouragement are lacking, an equally important kind of opportunity is the availability of peers who do value academic performance. Other aspects of the

---

[9] If one's interest is in individual differences, one may view the peer group as an agency that "normalizes" children who come from unusual backgrounds (Medinnus and Johnson, 1969). In fact, the school serves a similar function.

"opportunity structure" of our society will be considered in later chapters, but even at this early period in the child's life, it is apparent that socialization outcomes are influenced by the kinds of opportunities provided by the society. To the extent that these are different for people at different social levels, the socialization process and its outcomes will vary by social level.

The earlier discussion has suggested that the child from a poorer family is likely to be *more* in need of assistance from the school system than is the child from a higher social level. If the school is to be effective in its particular part of the socialization process, it must provide more of the basic motivation and more continuous assistance for children who do not receive such motivation and assistance at home. To say that this is what the schools *should* do, though, is to take what Wilson (1969, p. 82) has called the "radical conception of equality of opportunity:"

> The traditional liberal view of equality of opportunity which motivated the extension of public elementary and secondary education in this country would, as far as possible, remove legal and economic handicaps to the acquisition of education by intelligent and industrious youths whose parents sought their social advancement. The more radical conception calls for the provision of experiences which generate intelligence and arouse interest even where the influence of the home and neighborhood may be impoverished or hostile.[10]

There is little evidence that our society has made the kind of commitment to compensation for different backgrounds that would be necessary to increase the effectiveness of the school in this way. In fact, one of the critical social questions of the seventies is the extent to which the society *should* attempt, through the schools, to compensate for different family and neighborhood backgrounds. There is far from full agreement on this issue. Rejection of compensatory education comes from two opposite quarters. Those on the one side maintain that it is the family's obligation to prepare the child for the school experience, and though it is unfortunate if some families fail in that task, it is not the responsibility of the schools to correct that failure. From a different perspective, compensatory education is rejected as a subversive influence by which the dominant forces in the society can undercut the unique contributions of the family and of minority groups. The question of "equal opportunity," therefore, also involves questions about the "sanctity of the home" and the "right to be different." As a result, the school system, and the individual teacher within that system, is faced with conflicting expectations from different members of the society. It seems likely that the schools will exhibit signs of this conflict for some time to come.

---

[10] See also the chapters by J. S. Coleman and D. K. Cohen in the same volume.

five

ADOLESCENCE AND SECONDARY EDUCATION

As the title of the chapter suggests, the structure of the educational system and the biological development of the child correspond to a considerable extent. The onset of sexual maturity tends to occur about the time the child moves from elementary to secondary school, but variations are found both in the school system and in the rate of development of children. Some school systems involve only one point of transition, at the beginning of either the seventh or the ninth grade, the youngster then spending either four or six years in a single secondary school. Others involve two changes, first to junior high school, then to senior high school, three years being spent in each. Almost all children, however, experience a change of school at the end of the sixth or eighth grade. Somewhere during those years too, most children become sexually mature. At the same time, the biological maturation of children is quite varied. Some children, especially girls, may be sexually mature even before leaving elementary school, and other children, especially boys, may not reach sexual maturity until they are well into high school.

Such variation is the source of much "awkwardness" in the lives of American children because of the rather strict age-grading practiced by society and especially by the school. The awkwardness is reflected in relations within single-sex peer groups, in the relations between the two sexes, and in the school program itself. (Some junior high school teachers must attempt simultaneously to deal with "little boys" and sexually promiscuous girls.) The greater physical maturity of the girls tends to increase both sexes' awareness of sexual identity, and it accentuates the differentiation along sex lines that begins in the peer structure of the elementary school. It also introduces a factor that runs counter to the nondiscriminatory and age-graded principles of the school, since the greater maturity of girls leads them to associate with mature, thus older, boys. This general pattern, together with the great variation in age of sexual maturity among boys and girls, adds a new dynamic factor to the school and peer group experience.

These variations may be very significant in the socialization of individual children. The importance of sexual identity and the centrality of "pairing off" in the definition of full maturity in our society means that the biologically precocious child has a greater claim to maturity, both in his own eyes and in the view of his peers. Similarly, the slow-maturing child is presented with a problem in both self-conception and social relations. Such individual differences cannot be dealt with here in any systematic way. That sexual maturity occurs during secondary school and that it tends to occur among girls before it does among boys does have general implications for the socialization process in our society, however, and such implications will need to be considered in the later discussion.

Although biological changes may be the most dramatic ones during the years of secondary education, it is important to remember that a great deal more is going on. Adolescence, after all, is a period of life that is clearly recognized in our society; adolescents are viewed as different from both children and adults. Although Americans are not very explicit about the precise *nature* of the differences, either actual or desirable, adolescence is generally recognized as a period of change, of transition, of movement *toward* adulthood. The transitional nature of the period and the social and psychological elements of it are reflected in Campbell's (1969, pp. 822–23) rhetorical questions and answers:

> What, then, is supposed to happen during adolescence? How are adolescents supposed to behave and what experiences are they supposed to have? . . . First, adolescents are supposed to broaden substantially their range of social contacts and dramatically increase the number of others who are emotionally and normatively relevant to them by becoming less dependent on parents and home and more oriented to peers and to the adult world. Second, adolescents are supposed to experiment with what they are in relation to others in the sense of "trying on" new behaviors

and experiences, questioning themselves internally as to what they are and wish to be seen as, working toward integration of past experiences, present performances, and future expectancies, attaining a somewhat coherent, somewhat permanent answer to the question, "Who am I?" Third, adolescents are supposed to be learning to be adults, in the sense of acquiring social skills, selecting internal standards of judgment and conduct, and acquiring through practice in "make-believe" organizational settings (clubs, plays, school newspaper, student activities, etc.) the skills of constraint and presentation needed for success in the adult settings of an industrial, bureaucratized society. Fourth, the adolescent is widely viewed as being simultaneously in a suspended state of supreme frustration and in the middle of the best years of life.

This is a period of consolidation and testing, a time for self-examination and for a commitment to goals. Yet it is also a period of rejection of the past and a time for a critical assessment of the future. One is expected both to withdraw from adult society (by loosening the bond to one's parents) and to seek it out (through commitment to long-range goals). It is a time of increasing variety and opportunity, yet it is also a time when one begins to "feel the walls closing in."

These contradictions are in part a function of the fact that as autonomy and the pressures toward autonomy increase, the young person becomes increasingly aware of the long-range significance of his own qualities and of the nature of "the opportunity structure." As the individual becomes more independent of adult influences, he finds that such qualities as being pretty, smart, small, awkward, and so on make a difference in his ability to accomplish desired goals. He also finds not only that opportunities are not available to everyone, but also that choosing one alternative means bypassing another. Thus, one "must decide," but not all options are open, and one cannot do everything at once.

Much of what the child can take for granted becomes problematic for the adolescent. The organization of one's time and activities, the continued warm (or at least predictable) response of one's significant others, and the effectiveness of one's efforts to accomplish goals all present problems. Given a widening set of possible goals, an increased degree of self-determination, and a broadened social milieu, the adolescent has more need for active involvement and self-awareness. The "innocence" of childhood is in part due to adult protection and control; the "selfishness" of adolescence is a necessary part of accomplishing adult autonomy. In a very few years, the adolescent is required to put to use the results of his earlier socialization, decide how much he likes it (and how effective it is), and chart his course for the future. This does not, of course, happen all at once, but during the teen-age period he must become more aware of his own motives and values, attempt to function in accordance with them, and guide himself toward future goals. Thus, the outcomes of earlier socialization become more salient to the individual as he becomes a more active determiner of his own future. "Who am I?" and "Where am I going?" are questions he must face.

Changes in the social context within which the young person moves, in the kinds of socialization tasks he faces, and in the degree of his own contribution to the process all lead to a shift in his response to the three major socialization agencies. Equally clear, these changes require alterations in the way these agencies respond to him. The first three sections of this chapter examine the shifting relationship of the adolescent to his school, his peer group, and his family, respectively. The next three sections then analyze how the ways in which adolescents respond to the complex set of alternatives available to them influence their probable adult position in the stratification system.

The School

The secondary school provides a different social setting than the elementary school, a significant part of the difference being due to greater diversity and differentiation. In Chapter 4 it was noted that in elementary school a relatively homogeneous cohort of students tends to move through the first six grades together, one teacher assuming central importance at each grade level. This pattern is increasingly altered during the second six years of public school. The normal pattern is for several elementary schools to act as "feeders" to a single secondary school, junior high schools often acting as intermediary steps. To the extent that the several elementary schools have served neighborhoods with different social class, ethnic, or racial populations, the secondary school will have a much more diverse student body.[1]

Whatever the composition of the student body, the secondary school tends to provide a more differentiated curriculum than the elementary school and to present the student with a series of teachers during the school day. The relative importance of any one teacher is thereby reduced, and the student-teacher relationship tends to become more impersonal. Also, the set of courses and teachers experienced by any student may be quite different from that experienced by another. Not only may there be sections

---

[1] This is less likely to happen in very large cities, since such subpopulations may be large enough and residentially isolated enough to provide a rather homogeneous student body for even a large high school. This isolation results in what has been called *de facto* segregation at all grade levels and has been the basis for some to argue in favor of mass transportation of students to provide more diverse student bodies.

of some courses, owing to the large size of the student body in any grade, but these sections may be defined as being at different levels of academic difficulty. "Advanced placement" or "accelerated" sections may be available, and "slow" sections may be formed (though perhaps less publicized). In addition, not all students in the same grade will be taking the same courses. Electives will be available in addition to required courses. Some of these, like shop and home economics, will tend to segregate the sexes. Finally, in most high schools there is a rather clear differentiation of special "programs"—general, commercial, college preparatory, and so on—each having its own special curriculum.

The secondary school thus recognizes in its structure both the greater general autonomy of the adolescent and the diversity of interests, skills, and probable fates of its students. It also reflects the students' increasing involvement in "the real world." A number of courses are offered that have direct application in later life, such as woodworking, typing, and home economics. Other courses are supposed to give the student a better understanding of adult concerns: sex education, the study of government processes and current events, and so on.[2] Especially in the last few years of high school, students also have the opportunity to participate in various extracurricular activities that give them some limited practice in adult activities: the newspaper and yearbook, service organizations, clubs, and so on. Finally, the secondary school usually provides counseling for students in a more systematic way than does the elementary school. Among other things, secondary school counseling helps students make decisions about jobs and further education.

All these characteristics of secondary education promote the division of the student body into segments, each reflecting a set of common experiences, interests, and ambitions. There will be some tendency for those from the same neighborhood, those in the same academic program, those who participate in the same extracurricular activities, and so on, to form more intimate relations with each other and to separate themselves from others in the school. These subdivisions reflect the structure of the school program, and they also reflect the school's standards of evaluation. In most high schools, the value placed on higher education by the faculty leads to a reward system that favors the "advanced" sections and the college preparatory program. Although a variety of kinds of achievement are possible within the system, it is usually apparent that formal academic achievement is favored by school officials. Medals for outstanding performance in math and English, awards for science projects, and election to the National

---

[2] These courses are more likely than any others to be scorned by high school students as "Mickey Mouse." This attitude seems to result from adult ambivalence about "telling the whole truth" to young people as well as from pressure from various political and value-committed agencies. The students recognize the distortion and, as a result, the positive potential in such courses is often unrealized.

Honor Society are the most salient forms of recognition within the official system. It is unlikely that the outstanding typist, the skillful carpenter, or the creative chef will receive comparable recognition. As a result, student subgroups tend to be differentiated according to prestige.

The school does provide the context, and even some of the mechanisms, for achievement along other dimensions, however, and this is an important feature of secondary education. Some extracurricular activities are less academic than others, sports being the most obvious case in point. Recognition for successful participation in such activities is officially provided by the school, but it is usually apparent that such recognition causes strain within the system. Teachers in the academic subjects often complain about overemphasis on such activities, and the position of the coach in the faculty is often marginal. Yet, athletics, cheerleading, and playing in the band are unique kinds of activity for the student since they make him an official representative of the school, as symbolized by uniforms, the wearing of the school colors, and visible awards such as the varsity letters. The visibility of the activity and the active competition involved make the rewards even more attractive (Coleman, 1961).

A similar kind of visible recognition is possible through elected office. Popularity with one's peers is made manifest for a limited number of students in this way. The student who is sufficiently well known and well liked to be elected will probably have some appeal to various subdivisions of the student body, either through multiple activities (a good student *and* an athlete) or through exceptional personal qualities.

It is significant that of the two kinds of recognition given by the secondary school—academic and extra curricular—only the first can be found in the elementary school. In elementary school, the central concern is with the academic program; the school's emphasis is on motivating children for academic achievement and on the establishment of the knowledge and skill the child needs for further educational attainment. The only part of the secondary school program that clearly builds on this earlier experience is the academic program, especially the college preparatory program. Differentiation among the children on this purely academic dimension is well advanced by the time they reach secondary school. In large measure, it is already known which students are likely to go to college. The other programs (technical, commercial, general) are intended for those who "can't make it" in the college preparatory program. The implicit assumption is that those who have the ability will go into the college preparatory program, and conversely, those who do not go into the college preparatory program have less ability and need to be encouraged to have "lower horizons."[3]

---

[3] The definition of the school as an agency that matches up ability level and achievement level has led to a strong emphasis on testing and counseling. Those who do not "perform up to their ability level" are viewed as a serious problem, and considerable

Extracurricular achievement and even achievement in the "lesser" academic programs of the school are recognized by teachers and students alike as being less important than academic achievement. For the most part, only "good students" are rewarded by the school as a formal agency, and the nonacademic sources of reward within the school are unofficial, marginal, or even overtly demeaned by the school. As a result, the student entering secondary school has two rather distinct means of "making it." One is to continue to emphasize the criteria of success used in elementary school; the other is to stress those qualities that both the primary and secondary school define as academically irrelevant—athletics, popularity, and so on. The student who has been academically successful in elementary school has a smooth path to continued achievement. For the student who has been less successful, new options are opened. Only the first kind of student, however, can achieve wholly "within the system."

The adolescent's position makes him clearly aware of the imminence of adulthood, and one would expect that adult role models would thus assume greater importance at this time. The fact that adolescents spend so much time in school would also seem to make the teacher a likely role model. A number of factors reduce the teacher's significance as a model, however. First, since most of the contact a student has with any given teacher is limited to an hour a day (or less) in a highly structured classroom setting, there is little basis for a close student-teacher relationship. Second, since the official position of the teacher leads to an emphasis on academic standards, many students who question the significance of such standards will find the teacher an unattractive role model. Finally, the student's increasing awareness of the larger society leads him to realize that society has a rather low opinion of teachers. They are often viewed as rather ineffectual people, and in actuality they are not generally very potent in the world outside the school.[4] Such a view makes one's teachers rather unattractive models, especially in the case of boys in relation to their male teachers. Thus, although direct modeling of adult patterns tends to be salient in adolescence, and although teachers are among the most fully available adult models outside the family, even academically successful students may have reason to doubt the adequacy of the teacher as a model.[5]

---

time and energy is likely to be spent on dealing with the problem. This emphasis on matching ability and achievement level also leads to both subtle and overt pressures on students not to aspire beyond their presumed ability level. Thus, the secondary school not only *provides* various channels, it *influences* students to take the right one (Cicourel and Kitsuse, 1963).

[4] In this regard, it is noteworthy that the football coach, though not always highly regarded by the rest of the faculty, is often the best-known member of the faculty in the community.

[5] The fact that high school teachers are generally not among the top students in college (Davis, 1965) means that the better high school students may be academically

The Structure of Peer Relations

The need for greater independence from one's family, the emphasis on one's future, and the heightened significance of boy-girl relations all make the peer group an increasingly important part of the individual's life as he moves through the adolescent years (Bowerman and Kinch, 1959). The transition from being a child in the family of orientation to being an adult in the larger society is especially demanding in a society like ours. One moves from a small, intimate group in which one's relations are based on blood ties and an assumed mutual obligation and commitment into a complex, impersonal structure in which one's relations are based on achievement. Not only is the family unable to teach all one needs to know to be an effective adult, but it is also unable to provide the emotional support the young person requires during the period of transition to adulthood. The very need for independence as an adult requires that one must disengage oneself from one's parents and sibs. The peer group plays a very important role in easing the transition, providing a kind of "halfway house" to adulthood. Although emotional security within such a group cannot be assumed, and the peer group thus has some of the qualities of the larger society, the shared need for emotional support during this period of transition makes adolescents more responsive to each other than they were earlier (and than they will be later on). Also, the need to *achieve* this kind of supportive relationship, and the possibility of losing it, heightens one's awareness of his own relations with others and increases one's responsiveness to their praise and criticism.

The resulting close-knit clique structure and highly responsive concern for doing the "right" thing in the eyes of one's peers has led behavioral scientists to refer to a distinct "adolescent society" and "youth culture." Although some sort of "youth culture" is undoubtedly inevitable in any society in which the family does not provide a fully adequate base for adult functioning (Eisenstadt, 1956), other aspects of our society encourage a rather extreme version. The age-graded organization of the school system and the extended period of education require that young people spend a large part of their waking hours together. We literally segregate them from the rest of the society and its activities. In addition, there is a consistent emphasis within the society on the importance of youth and on the fact that the adolescent years are the "best years of your life," an emphasis that encourages the peer group to develop its own unique qualities. Finally, the

---

more talented than their teachers. Thus, even in terms of the very standards the teacher promotes, he may be an inadequate model for those who excel in terms of those standards.

pattern of rapid social change in America highlights the inadequacy of current standards for life in the society of the future. There is thus a general feeling (even among older people) that the younger generation will have to "make it on its own" under conditions we can only dimly foresee.

The peer group is thus not only an important structural part of the socialization process, providing a mechanism of transition from dependent childhood to independent adulthood, but it also acquires an organization and a set of norms and values of its own. Its organization is relatively "flat," with little power differentiation tolerated. This characteristic is consistent with the general rejection of adult involvement and with the questioning of adult standards. Evaluation of others is based on their personal attractiveness and adherence to in-group norms. Reciprocity and mutuality are highly valued. The norms and values that are most obvious are quite distinct from those of the larger society. The continual emphasis on excitement, glamour, and having a good time; the distinctive language, clothing, and music; the positive value placed on "doing nothing"; the joyous violation of adult norms (by speeding, using alcohol and drugs, experimentation with sex, violating parental and school rules, and so on), all of these set the youth culture apart.

Yet the contrast between youth culture and adult culture may give a false impression of the homogeneity of the peer group. In fact, adolescent society is as clearly differentiated as is adult society. Every high school has several "crowds," which tend to be mutually exclusive and even antagonistic to each other. Being in the "right crowd" is a very important matter for the adolescent. In general, these sub-groups tend to reflect the structure of the school itself, each one tending to involve students at similar social class and academic performance levels (Coleman, 1961; Turner, 1964). Not all of these subgroups are oriented in the same way to adults. In some cases, the norms of such a group will be overtly antagonistic to anything adults seem to value; but in others, the group promotes what seems to be a caricature of adult patterns; and in still others, there will be a close correspondence between the group's norms and those of adults. A simple typology of "delinquents," "swingers," and "squares," though, does not adequately reflect the variety found. The fact that the parents and the school officials may not espouse the same values, for instance, provides a basis for further differentiation depending on the cliques' views of these two sets of adults.

Sex role socialization is another important function of the peer group. Earlier socialization experiences (in the family, in school, and elsewhere) consistently acknowledge the differences between the sexes and selectively encourage specific sex-appropriate values, attitudes, goals, and behavior. There is no other social setting besides the adolescent peer group, however, in which the individual is called upon to enact (at the same time he is learning) the direct interpersonal portions of one's sex role. One has had some opportunity in other settings to observe very limited (and usually somewhat unreal) examples of those portions of the sex role—in one's parents' behavior, through the movies and TV, and so on—but for the most part one learns by doing. To the extent one has "teachers" or "coaches," they tend to be one's age-mates of the same sex who evolve normative patterns for such relations within the general context of basic moral definitions that the youngsters have, for the most part, learned within the family. Such norms are enforced by the threat of ostracism from the clique (Coleman, 1961; Douvan and Adelson, 1966). There is also, of course, a constant flow of cross-sex experience, which acts as a basis for assessing these norms. Thus, within any set of interacting boys and girls a cross-sex normative consensus will probably be established regarding such interactions.[6]

The centrality of boy-girl relations, and the evolution of normative consensus among peers about such relations, is thus another basis of division within the total peer group. Somewhat different definitions of acceptable boy-girl relations will evolve within different cliques ("the fast crowd" is identifiable in any high school). Not only degree of sexual permissiveness (Rainwater, 1966; Reiss, 1960) but styles of dating behavior and definitions of what is "fun" will vary. So will the degree of formality of boy-girl relations: Is going steady silly or necessary for one's self-esteem? The clique structures within the peer group will be formed in part on such issues.

To refer to *the* adolescent society and *the* youth culture, therefore, is an oversimplification, at least so far as the social structure of the peer group and the norms and values it espouses are concerned. The important *general* characteristic of the peer group, however, is its role in clarifying and solidifying the individual's view of himself and his definition of the larger society into which adolescents see themselves moving. There is a tendency for subgroups to be formed by youngsters who already have had common experiences and who share values. The importance of peer experiences in their lives generates strong pressures for social conformity and promotes an even greater degree of homogeniety within the clique. The peer group thus becomes differentiated into cliques that selectively reinforce varying definitions of adolescence and of the relationship between the individual and society. Although a common social reinforcement process occurs in all such subgroups, widely different kinds of norms and values are being reinforced,

---

[6] The general cultural definition of the male as the initiator and the female as the controller of these relations provides the basis for tension in boy-girl relations. If there were not an underlying consensus between the sexes, however, the relations would be much more chaotic than they are.

and such differences have implications for both present action and future possibilities.[7]

The Adolescent and His Family

The school and the peer group provide the adolescent with most of his experience with the "outside world," and his involvement with them is both temporally extensive and personally absorbing. By comparison, his involvement in the family is very limited. In a very real sense, the youngster moves gradually out of his family of orientation during adolescence. He spends less time at home, he is less interested in family activities, and he actively seeks to establish a social position for himself that is independent of his family. Conversely, his parents are progressively less able to monitor his activities, and direct control becomes less and less possible. The most his parents can do is to prescribe a schedule for his activities (be home for meals, adhere to a curfew, and so on). They can ask for reports on what he does when he is away, but such a request is not likely to be very effective ("Where did you go?" "Nowhere." "What did you do?" "Nothing."). The general recognition that this is a period of maturation and preparation for adult independence leads most parents and children to view reduced involvement with the family as normal, necessary, and even desirable. The family does not lose its significance in the adolescent's life, however. The fact that the adolescent is moving out from a family of orientation that has particular characteristics, and the fact that this reduced involvement occurs over time rather than all at once, makes the youngster's relationship with his parents and siblings a very significant one.

Much of the literature on adolescence emphasizes parent-child conflict. It often oversimplifies the changing relationship between parent and child, however. The change is toward greater independence on the part of the child, and greater concern for his peers. This change requires an alteration in the behavior of both parent and child as well as an acceptance by both that such a change is desirable. There seems little doubt that American parents generally *want* their adolescents to become independent. "Altogether, it seems reasonable to interpret most parent-adolescent conflict as occurring not because the direction of the adolescent's quest for greater independence is illegitimate but because perfect congruence in the speed

---

[7] The further differentiation according to the individual's position *within* such a subgroup is also highly significant, of course. Being a leader or one who is simply tolerated undoubtedly influences one's own view of his place in society, whatever the value orientation of the subgroup.

and circumstance under which new forms of expression are tolerable is not achieved" (Campbell, 1969, p. 830). Much of the awkwardness of adolescence in our society derives from the lack of clarity in the definition of this change process. The awkwardness is experienced by both the adolescent and his parents, and it leads to some conflict in most families and very severe conflict in some.

The level of conflict is not nearly so great as any simple peers-versus-parents perspective would suggest, however. One of the reasons for this, of course, is that parents are not in a position to know the full extent to which their children's behavior deviates from what they would wish it to be, and this ignorance has a damping effect on conflict (Moore and Tumin, 1949). At least as important, however, is the fact that the family's influence in the early socialization of the child continues to be felt. Adolescents have rather firm value commitments, and these have been strongly influenced by their parents. Parent-child consensus on basic values is thus common. Also, although peer values are certainly crucial with regard to some issues, these tend to be issues that are of immediate rather than long-term relevance (Brittain, 1963; Sebald, 1968), and adolescents still tend to look to parents for guidance regarding decisions that will affect them as adults (Kandel and Lesser, 1969).

In most cases, parents continue to be very significant, but the degree of influence from parents as compared with peers during this period seems to be highly variable. There is evidence that the self-image of the adolescent tends to correspond with (and thus is presumably influenced by) his parents' view of him (Wylie, 1961), and it has been found (Douvan and Adelson, 1966) that more American adolescents name their mother or father as their adult ideal than name any other person. But it is also true that the degree to which youngsters use their parents as models varies with the quality of the parent-child relationship. In keeping with the discussion in Chapters 2 and 3, an adolescent is more likely to model himself after a democratic parent who explains the reasons for his or her requests (Elder, 1963).

Such findings do not, of course, suggest that peers are unimportant in the life of the adolescent. The peer group provides an alternative to the family. In fact, poor relations with the family appear to be associated with increased dependence upon one's peers (Bowerman and Kinch, 1959). It seems appropriate, therefore, to view the family and the peer group as two sources of influence that generally tend to be complementary but that have the potential for conflict. The isolated and encapsulated nature of peer relations is such that if the child does not bring to these relations a rather firm commitment to basic values, or if the child's relations with his parents are badly strained, he may accept peer influences that run contrary to those of his parents. Although this is not a general pattern, the potential is there.

One further source of family influence needs to be mentioned, although there has, unfortunately, been almost no investigation of it. Most adolescents have one or more siblings, and relations with siblings are undoubtedly of considerable importance during this period. It seems obvious that an older sibling, especially one of the same sex, might act as a significant model for the adolescent, assuming that there is a positive relationship between them. Similarly, it seems likely that an older sibling might take an interest in the younger one and provide at least intermittant guidance. Even a sibling of the opposite sex can be very important in this way, given the significance of cross-sex relations and the need to understand what the other sex is like. The adolescent with younger siblings might similarly be expected to provide a model (and possibly act as a teacher) for the younger children. What it's like to be an adolescent or to be a young adult, then, can be learned in part within the pattern of sibling relations. Some of the literature on sex role development and on differences by birth order suggests the importance of such relations (Sutton-Smith and Rosenberg, 1970), but little explicit study of their effects has been done. For our purposes, it may be sufficient to note that this is a further reason to emphasize the continuing importance of family relations during the adolescent period.

Differentiation and Commitment

The three major socialization agencies—family, school, peers—all continue to be important in adolescence, but the nature of their influence is different from what it was in childhood. The increasingly diverse set of social relations open to the youngster, together with the greater independence he seeks (and is accorded), alter the pattern. The lowered ability of the parents to monitor and control the adolescent's behavior means that meaningful involvement with them is largely of his own choosing. However, his family is also "built into" him in the form of values and motives. The school, though still a very significant part of his day-to-day experience, and still a promoter of academic values, offers him an increasingly diverse set of options. Although the options are not all equally valued by the school, they are at least presented as legitimate channels of personal investment. The most significant test of the young person's evolving independence is provided by the peer group. In that context, he is more on his own, the definitions of excellence are less explicit, and "success" is less predictable. The relative isolation of the peer group from adult influence, together with the diversity of its members (and the cliques they form), provide him with his initial challenge to make decisions, to choose alternatives—and to suffer the consequences.

Within this matrix of social relations there occurs a sorting process that has its origins in infancy and childhood and that has far-reaching effects in adulthood. The variety of cliques offers the adolescent a potential for significant social relations with youngsters who emphasize rather different values and motives and who vary in the kinds of knowledge and skill they have acquired. One chooses and is chosen by some of these, and rejects and is rejected by others. The selection process tends to be based on similarity of values and attitudes, each clique tending to be homogeneous. The "openness" of the structure increases the pressures toward clique homogeneity, since acceptance and rejection are always optional. One is always being put to the test, at least implicitly: Are you one of us or not? Are you with us or against us? In the process of meeting such a challenge, especially when the options are widely different, the individual is faced with the question, "Who am I?" in a forceful way. Since the choices involved are not wholly his own, however, the answer to the question is, in part, provided by others. If he defines himself differently from the way they define him, it will require considerable personal commitment to maintain his self-definition in the face of the contrary social pressure (Newcomb, 1961).[8]

Although the sorting process occurs within the peer group, it is strongly influenced by both the school and the family. Although the family's influence is largely felt through the kinds of values and motives the child has acquired, such influence continues to exist. The quality of the youngster's relations with his family, especially his parents, will influence his relations with his peers. The degree to which he cares about his parents' reactions to his behavior will influence that behavior, whatever his own values may be. If he feels a close relation with his parents, he may do things or refrain from doing things because he doesn't want to hurt them. Similarly, if his relations with them are badly strained, he may explicitly engage in activities he knows they will not like, as a form of revenge. It is also likely that an adolescent's relations with his siblings will influence his behavior in a similar way—he may try to show off to them, set a good example, or attempt to live up to their image of him. The family thus continues to be a significant social reference point, and one's relations within the family will influ-

---

[8] In the usual case, the match between self-definition and the view of one's peers is probably reasonably close, but the extreme case can occur and is potentially very stressful. The "kid from across the tracks" who has been successfully socialized into an acceptance of middle-class values may suffer from rejection by those who espouse these values at the same time he is being defined as "potentially one of us" by his neighborhood delinquent gang. The cross-pressures from such a mismatch between value commitment and social acceptance can be very disturbing at any age, but they are particularly so when the individual is already facing the considerable challenge of adolescence in a society like ours.

ence how he responds to the options presented to him outside the family.

The school has an even more tangible influence on the sorting process. Although the school provides a number of optional channels for the individual, these are not equally available to all students, and the school attempts to guide its students into the "right" channels. This is most obvious in the sorting of students into the several academic programs. Not everyone can enter the college preparatory program, and some who may seek to enter it are encouraged to alter their course, either through counseling or through regulations that require previous achievements for a student to gain admission. Even without such selective devices, though, many students choose other options because by the time they get to high school they have been convinced that they are not very talented academically. Entering the college preparatory program would only be "asking for more trouble." Various selection devices are also used to limit students' participation in other options provided by the school. One must perform academically at a certain level in order to take part in extracurricular activities, and one may be barred from participation if one violates the social regulations of the school. Finally, more indirect or subtle factors tend to discourage the participation of some students in such optional activities. Students who ride the school bus cannot take part in after-school activities; coaches insist that athletes have haircuts; clubs select their members by rather vague criteria; and so on.

Students therefore choose some options themselves, and are themselves selected by various devices within the school system itself. Such distribution means that any individual student interacts much more with some of his fellow students than he does with others. Also, those who interact tend to be defined as "belonging together" according to the system of relations of the school. "The brains," "the jocks," "the dummies," and "the big wheels" can all be identified both by their individual performances and by their associations with others who are like them. Distribution within the school system thus provides the base for the establishment of cliques, and such cliques tend to reinforce the definition of their members as distinctive, both to outsiders and to themselves.

This sorting process occurs with adulthood on the horizon. The nature of the larger society is becoming increasingly apparent to the adolescent, and he cannot avoid knowing something about the kind of place he is likely to occupy within it. His image of adulthood may be fuzzy or distorted, but he has both an image and an attitude toward it, and he has a view of how his current situation is related to adulthood. The varying patterns of behavior within the high school reflect both this view of the adult future and the definition of the current situation, which involves the school with its academic and extracurricular activities as well as those activities that constitute the youth culture.

There are highly diverse ways in which an adolescent can be oriented to the current situation as well as toward adulthood. Table 5.1 suggests a very limited number of these possibilities in oversimplified form. It is over-simplified in two ways. First, in each case, only a positive or a negative orientation is suggested. However, any individual may express degrees of favorability and respond differently to different parts of the activities re-ferred to in each column. Second, not all possible combinations of positive and negative orientations are recorded in the table. A total of sixteen types, using the plus and minus signs, is possible, but the eight types shown seem to be most common and are more easily recognized.

TABLE 5.1
A Typology of High School Students

Type	Orientations to Current and Future Activities			
	Academic Performance	Extracurricular Activities	Youth Culture Activities	Adult Role Performance
All-American	+	+	+	+
Square	+	+	−	+
Immature Conformist	+	+	+	−
Grind	+	−	−	+
Big Wheel	−	+	+	+
Escapist	−	+	+	−
Dropout	−	−	+	+
Rebel	−	−	+	−

Most of the types noted in Table 5.1 are sufficiently obvious and familiar not to require much comment. The important general point to be made about these types, though, is that they reflect selection from among the multiplicity of options open to the high school student. The student who "makes it" academically is likely to remain positively oriented to academic performance, but his academic performance is only one part of the picture. If he pours himself wholly into that kind of activity, he will not participate in those maturing kinds of associations with his peers that prepare him for the give and take of adult social relations. Even if he has a positive view of adult roles (the "grind"), his preparation for such roles is likely to be incomplete. If the peer relations he does experience are wholly within the context of adult supervision (the "square"), he may also find it threaten-ing to engage in a more open competitive adult relationship. In both of these cases, however, the youngster is at least positively oriented to adult roles. The adolescent who wholly immerses himself in the activities of the present, without a positive orientation to future roles, is likely to be even more poorly prepared for adulthood (the "immature conformist"). The implications of the present for the future, and the necessity to prepare for that future, will be avoided.

The student who is not positively oriented to academic performance similarly has a number of options. He may maintain his position within the school system by engaging in extracurricular activities (assuming a minimum level of academic performance), and orient himself to the future via the social elements of his present situation (the "big wheel"). In many students, however, a negative attitude toward academic work is associated with such low levels of performance that there is literally nothing in the school for them. Such individuals may rebel against the school as a means of socialization and attempt to move rapidly into adult roles (the "dropout") or they may reject the whole adult-dominated society (the "rebel").[9]

A dual process of selection and reinforcement tends to occur within the clique structure of the peer group. Those with similar values and attitudes tend to form cliques, and the social relations within the cliques act as sources of influence to reinforce the commitment to those values and attitudes. In this way, cliques legitimate kinds of behavior that may affect the members' relations with both the family and the school as well as having implications for their future options. Whether or not one does his homework, violates parental curfews, engages in delinquent behavior, disrupts the classroom, takes part in "serious" extracurricular activities, or engages in community service projects will depend heavily on what activities the clique approves of. Positive and negative sanctions are used by clique members to encourage behavior in accordance with shared values, the ultimate negative sanction being ostracism.

Engaging in clique-approved behavior determines what kind of relationship one will have with one's parents and teachers, thus affecting the kind of influence these adults will have on the individual. Such behavior also opens or closes access to further options. For example, failure to perform academically at an earlier point not only makes one less *able* to perform later but also leads to one's not being provided with the *opportunity* to do so. There are many other instances of progressive narrowing of options.

---

[9] Those familiar with Merton's (1957) analysis of anomie will recognize the similarity between the present discussion and his analysis. In fact, he uses the rejection of adult values and immersion in the youth culture as an example of rebellion (p. 191). The present discussion deals with a somewhat more complex typology, because it is necessary to take into account the adolescent's orientation to both the youth culture and the society's values as reflected in the school and adult roles. Merton discusses acceptance and rejection of socially approved values in combination with acceptance and rejection of socially approved means of achieving those values. Within that framework, academic performance and, to a lesser degree, extracurricular participation are socially approved means of achieving adult values. Both the "grind" and the "big wheel" are using socially approved means to achieve those values, whereas the "dropout" is using socially disapproved means to achieve the same values, and the "rebel" is rejecting both the means and the values.

The youngster who has gotten into trouble with the police may find his teachers less willing to give him another chance to show his academic potential. The boy whose clique values a "hippie" style may be seen by the football coach as having less talent than others. The girl who emphasizes sex appeal in her dress and manner may fail to get the part in the school play. The youngster whose clique's "real living" begins at midnight may find that his parents are not very helpful when he needs money for a special project. Such experiences lead to a withdrawal from some relationships and activities and a further emphasis on others. They not only cut off certain possibilities, they lead the clique to define such possibilities as undesirable. In this way, the differentiation within the peer group tends to solidify value commitments and to point clique members toward (and away from) various pathways into adulthood.

One of the major pathways with far-reaching implications in adult life is educational attainment. Though it is not the only factor determining adult social status in our society, it is extremely important. As is suggested by the above, academic performance is intimately related to other kinds of activities during adolescence. The next section reviews briefly the evidence relating to the explanation of varying levels of academic performance in high school. As might be expected, the evidence suggests that academic performance is influenced both by what the youngster "brings to" the high school in the form of values, knowledge, motives, and skills and by the experiences he has during high school.

Levels of Academic Performance

The most obvious place to look for an explanation for varying levels of academic performance is in the differences in intellectual ability. There is, of course, a sizeable relationship between measures of intelligence and measures of academic performance (Lavin, 1965, Chapter 4), but it is far from perfect. One must go beyond measures of intelligence if one is to explain the wide range of academic performance in high school.[10]

---

[10] Using intelligence as a source of explanation of academic performance is in itself filled with difficulties. Performance on tests of intelligence, it can be argued, is influenced by one's experience as well as one's native ability. Perhaps Coleman, Campbell, et al. (1966) put it about as bluntly as anyone when they said: "The ability tests [used in their study] have been in the past, and are often still, termed 'intelligence tests' or 'IQ tests,' and seen as measures of more fundamental and stable mental abilities, but recent research does not support that view. Ability tests are simply broader and more general measures of education, while achievement tests are narrower measures directed to a restricted subject area. The findings of this survey provide additional evidence that the 'ability' tests are at least as much affected by school differences as are the 'achievement' tests" (pp. 292–93).

One of the most consistent correlates of academic performance is social status, a finding that persists even when intelligence level is controlled (Lavin, 1965). Among students at a given level of I.Q., low-status students tend on the average to perform at a lower level than high-status students. In Chapter 4 it was suggested that differences in academic performance tend to increase during the elementary grades owing to the cumulative nature of the school's teachings. Although the varying programs offered in the high school tend to absorb some of these differences by providing different kinds of academic challenge, the relationship between performance and social class continues to be found (Coleman, Campbell, et al., 1966).

Other findings help to put this general relationship between social class and academic performance into a more meaningful context. For instance, Coleman, Campbell, et al., (1966) found a variable that they called "control of environment" to be consistently related to both academic achievement and social class.[11] Such a measure reflects both the individual's sense of potency and the degree to which he sees experience as predictable and controllable. Lower-class students generally score lower on "control of environment" and also perform less well academically. Other investigators have found similar measures to be associated with academic performance, holding intelligence constant (Strodtbeck, 1958).[12] In all these studies, lower-class adolescents saw the environment as less controllable and performed less well in school than did middle-class students.

Closely related are findings from studies that used various personality measures. For instance, Rosen (1956) has pointed up a three-way relationship among social class, academic performance, and achievement motivation, the latter being a measure of the need to excel in relation to standards of excellence of any kind. Students who have high achievement motivation tend to come from higher social class levels, and they tend to perform better in school. Measures of autonomy and persistence in task performance

---

[11] The measure consisted of three agree-disagree items: "Good luck is more important than hard work for success," "Every time I try to get ahead, something or somebody stops me," and "People like me don't have much of a chance to be successful in life." Much of the analysis using this measure was directed toward understanding performance differences by race. Further reference to that aspect of the analysis will be made in the Appendix.

[12] In most studies such variables are referred to as "achievement values." Such measures usually involve one or more of three kinds of statements: (1) that it is possible to manipulate the environment, (2) that there is justification in delaying immediate pleasure for the sake of long-range goals, and (3) that one should not let ties to one's family interfere with getting ahead in the world. Kahl (1965) has discussed the relationships among such measures. An additional dimension of importance is the degree to which the individual sees opportunities open to him that the society defines as legitimate. Lower-class boys are more likely than middle-class boys to see fewer of these and to see more opportunities that the society defines as illegitimate (Short, Rivera, and Tennyson, 1965).

also seem to be related both to social class level and to academic performance (Douvan and Adelson, 1958; MacArthur, 1955; McDavid, 1959). Students who have the ability to work independently and persistently toward their goals perform better; such students also come more often from higher-status families.

These findings all correspond to expectations based on the discussion in the earlier chapters of this volume. It was noted there that lower-status parents see the world in much the same way as these low performance students do. Such parents also tend to relate to their children in such a way that their children are less likely than others to develop high levels of achievement motivation or to internalize a set of standards that will serve as a dependable guide to long-range goal striving. Such children also tend to perform less well in school and thus are more likely to experience failure. An expected outcome of such failure is that the young person may avoid committing himself to strive for success in the future. The view of one's environment as not controllable, which such students learn from their parents, is confirmed by their own experience in school. Both the family and the school, therefore, provide bases for the development in lower-class children of qualities that have been shown to be related to low levels of academic performance.

The social context within which the individual spends his adolescence is as important as the personal qualities he has developed earlier, however. What kind of high school he goes to, for instance, makes a great deal of difference. Schools vary in the degree to which they are academically oriented, and those with more academic climates have students who perform better and who have higher aspirations (McDill, Rigsby, and Meyers, 1969). Such differences in climate seem to reflect wider community interest in education, especially the interest exhibited by parents. The adolescent's own parents' encouragement seems to make a significant difference for his views of education and his aspirations for the future (Sewell and Shah, 1968). The makeup of the student body is another important part of the social context. Lower-status students with many higher-status classmates tend to do better in school (Coleman, Campbell, et al., 1966) than those without such classmates, and those whose best friends have high educational aspirations are more likely to have high aspirations also (Alexander and Campbell, 1964). Greater involvement in even the nonacademic parts of the school program also seems to increase one's level of educational aspiration (Rehberg and Schafer, 1968).[13]

---

[13] High aspirations may not always be a good thing, however. Inability to achieve one's aspired-to level may lead to a rejection of the whole educational enterprise (Stinchcombe, 1965) as well as a lowered faith in legitimate means of "getting ahead" in the society (Han, 1968).

Such findings suggest that there will be no simple one-to-one relationship between social class of origin and either academic performance or level of educational attainment. Although there are general class-related bases for the development of the personal characteristics just discussed, and although lower-class students do tend to go to school together and do tend to have less encouragement from their parents, there is a great deal of variation. Within any social level there are many different kinds of parents and schools.[14] Varying combinations of these factors will produce a variety of outcomes.

Variations by Sex

With the onset of adolescence, sexual identity becomes highly significant in the view of both the individual and those around him. Although efforts are made in the elementary school to maintain a uniform program regardless of sex, in high school the program is more diversified, in part to accommodate the different interests of boys and girls. The differences between the sexes go well beyond those allowed for in the program, however. Most of the relationships between performance and other variables discussed in the previous section are found more clearly with boys than with girls. There seems to be a more consistent relationship among girls between measures of ability and academic performance (Lavin, 1965), and other variables such as those just discussed explain less about their differences in performance. Such sex differences must be seen in the context of the changing situation as youngsters move through adolescence.

In Chapter 4 it was noted that the fact that the great majority of elementary school teachers are women influences the child's school experience. The elementary school emphasis on orderliness, taking turns, being considerate of others, and giving the "right" answer fits more fully the society's definition of feminine than of masculine modes of behavior. A "real boy" may well feel the need to reject the good-student role in order to confirm his own masculinity (Parsons, 1949). Not surprisingly, therefore, it is found that girls tend to perform at a superior level in elementary school (Hughes, 1953). Since girls fit more easily into the school setting and their normal sex-role characteristics better equip them for performance in that setting, there is less reason to expect their personal characteristics to influence that performance to a significant extent.

---

[14] Some of the variations within working-class populations and their significance for the aspirations of working-class adolescents are discussed by Kahl (1953) and by Krauss (1964).

As they get older, the school as a socialization agency takes on different meaning for both boys and girls. The basic cultural expectation that the boy will become a full-time participant in the labor force, together with the close relationship between educational attainment and occupational placement, gives academic performance a much more instrumental meaning for boys than for girls. Boys generally feel much more pressure to do well in secondary school than do girls, a pressure that is increasingly felt as the boy gets older. Girls, on the other hand, are encouraged to direct their attention to the boy-girl relationship because the adult woman's social position depends upon that of her husband. An emphasis on the sexual elements in her sex-role is also encouraged by the earlier and more dramatic changes girls experience at puberty. As youngsters enter adolescence, therefore, boys are more likely to be concerned about achievement and girls to be concerned about their personal characteristics and how well they are accepted by others (Sexton, 1969). This concern for social relations seems to be related to the fact that the level of academic performance drops at puberty for many girls, especially the more talented ones (Shaw and McCuen, 1960; Maccoby, 1966). In fact, the favorableness of the self-image of adolescent girls seems much more dependent on their image of their personal qualities than the boy's self-image, which depends more upon intellectual qualities (Shaw, Edson, and Bell, 1960).

Such differences suggest that boys, more than girls, experience a strain between the need to perform well in school and the set of conditions under which that performance is possible. As boys mature, they become increasingly aware of the importance of education in their future, but they also become increasingly aware of the significance of past achievements for present and future academic performance. Those who have performed reasonably well in the past may feel increased concern for schoolwork and preparation for the future during adolescence. Those who have not done well in the past and who do not foresee the possibility of doing well in high school may seek other avenues of achievement. Some will find these avenues within the more varied high school experience—in athletics, social leadership, and such. For others, the options may be more limited, and they will tend to rebel through greater participation in the youth culture (Sugarman, 1967) or may actually leave school.

These sex-related patterns will vary by social class for several reasons. As reported in Chapter 4, lower-status children are likely to have done less well in elementary school. The probability of adequate performance in high school for such youngsters is thus not very high. The sense of the futility of high school work is likely to be strong, especially for boys. There is also the general problem of authority relations faced by all adolescents, but especially by lower-class boys. Independence striving among lower-class boys seems to reflect an attempt to escape from authority rather than an attempt to accompish personal goals (Douvan and Adelson, 1966; Goldstein, 1967). Rejection of adult authority may even lead the student who has the capability to fail to perform adequately in the adult-dominated school setting. Finally, the greater sexual promiscuity among lower-status adolescents (Rainwater, 1966) directs the attention of both boys and girls to other aspects of the adult role and makes the official school definition of boy-girl relations appear to be "immature" and unacceptable. All of these factors tend to lead the lower-class adolescent, especially the boy, away from the school as a source of meaningful experience. For many, in fact, the school becomes a constant reminder of inadequacy. Leaving such a situation is bound to have its appeal, and extending education beyond high school is likely to seem both impossible and unattractive.

Looking Ahead

For our purposes, the significance of the process of differentiation and of the varying levels of academic performance lies in their effects on the adolescent's future. Clearly, what happens in the high school years pretty well determines the level of education the individual will attain, and that level of education is strongly related to his adult position in the stratification system. As a result, it is tempting to think in terms of a simple straight-line causal sequence running from the individual's social class of origin to his social class of destination: Low social origin exposes the child to "inadequate" early socialization, which leads to poor academic performance in elementary school, which leads to rejection of academic values in high school which leads to a low level of education, which finally leads to low adult status. There is certainly evidence that such a sequence occurs in many cases. In fact, the existence of such a sequence is the best basis we have to explain the actual degree of continuity from level of origin to level of destination.

It would be a mistake to view such a sequence as universally valid, however, and it would be equally mistaken to emphasize the academic side of the individual's experience exclusively. The critical features of the adolescent experience are that it occurs in a relatively "open" society (one in which multiple options are available) and that it is so strongly influenced by one's peers. The options that are open are not all academic ones by any means, and the peer influences involved are highly diverse in nature. Close ties with peers fulfill a need generated by the social requirement that one leave the intimate environment of the family of orientation and move into a more complex and impersonal social environment. The potential for change in basic values and motives from such close ties with others is undoubtedly significant. Even more significant, however, is their potential for influence on the individual's behavior, and his behavior may have long-term consequences.

Such long-term consequences may ensue from behavior that is not at all directly related to academic performance. Having a police record, getting a girl "in trouble" (or being that girl), doing anything that seriously strains one's relations with one's parents—all these can significantly alter one's future. Such things may be more likely to happen to youngsters in some social classes, and some social classes may have more resources for dealing with such problems once they occur, but they are not wholly class-bound by any means. Testing the limits, falling in love, and wanting to be mature are common at all social levels, and are likely to lead to behavior that can seriously affect one's later life. In short, although adolescent activities are not fully oriented toward the future, what one does in the present may well influence that future.

The most important part of that future, for our purposes, is the social level the individual will occupy as an adult. For men, this is defined according to the occupation they assume; for women, it is usually defined by the occupation of their husbands. For both sexes education is an important determiner of adult social level. Becoming an adult thus consists of completing one's education, getting a job, and getting married. Although not everyone does those things in the same order, they are the most obvious indications that adolescence is over and the individual is an adult. The next chapter examines these changes in the lives of young Americans.

six

ENTERING ADULTHOOD

One of the sources of difficulty in adolescence in this country is that we do not clearly define the point at which a person becomes an adult. A whole series of significant points mark his entry into adulthood for specific purposes, but these range over at least a five-year period, from age 16 to age 21. The age at which one may leave school, drive a car, drink beer or hard liquor, get drafted, get married without his parent's permission, sign a legal document, and vote may all be different, and may even vary from state to state. Using only age as an indication, most people would agree that a person is an adult when he is 21, but many would insist that adulthood is reached before that age, and a few might argue for an older age.

From the perspective of the socialization process, most of these age-based marks of adulthood are less significant than other, less uniform indices. Since we view socialization as a process by which the individual is prepared to carry out the duties of adult positions in society, the mark of adulthood most significant for our purposes is the actual performance of adult roles. Given the high degree of differentiation within the adult population of this society, not all adults have the same tasks, and thus "being an adult" is a rather different matter for different segments of the population. Two positions, however, are almost universally assumed by adults in our society. The first, which is equally common for men and women, is the position of marriage partner; the second, which is much more common among men, is the position of worker. Whatever one's age, being married or having a full-time job requires the individual to perform adult roles. For purposes of this discussion, therefore, entry into these two positions will be used as an indication of adulthood.

Also, since full-fledged participation in the adult activities of the society calls for "doing" or "being" rather than "preparing," an additional index of adulthood is the completion of activities that are clearly preparatory. Although one's education may continue after marriage and entry into the labor force, this is not the usual pattern, and completion of one's education terminates one of the most important preparatory processes in an individual's life. Since level of education is closely linked with one's adult prestige, the point at which one terminates his education also has very significant implications for the *kinds* of adult positions he occupies.

Entering adulthood will thus be defined here as leaving school, getting a job, and getting married. People sometimes go back to school much later, change jobs, or leave their first marriage relationship, but these are all variations within a general process to be reviewed here. They all occur within the context of adult responsibilities, and it is the first experience of those responsibilities that we need to examine. In all three cases, it will be important for us to consider variations by social class and by sex.

Leaving School

Even ignoring the unusual cases in which an individual returns to some form of schooling after he is well into middle age, the point at which people leave school is extremely variable. The high school dropout may leave at 16, and the graduate or professional student may still be in school at 25 or even later. The vast majority of students complete the ninth grade in school, but after that point there is rapid attrition. It has been estimated that of 1,000 students who were in the fifth grade in 1960, 966 completed the ninth grade, 853 completed the eleventh grade, 721 graduated from high school, approximately 400 went to college, and only about 200 will graduate from college (Simon and Grant, 1967). Another way of viewing this variation is to examine the distribution of educational attainment of young adults. For instance, 23 percent of young Americans 25 to 29 years of age have not completed high school, 45 percent have completed high school but have gone no further, and only 19 percent have graduated from college (U.S. Census, P-20, No. 194).[1] For present purposes, however, the more crucial question is *which* people complete various levels of education.

Overall, the high school dropout rate does not vary appreciably by sex, although there may be a slight tendency for girls who drop out to do so at a somewhat earlier age than boys. In 1969, for instance, 7.2 percent of the boys and 9.1 percent of the girls 16 and 17 years of age were not in school and had not graduated from high school. In the same year, however, 14.9 percent of the boys and 15.2 percent of the girls 18 and 19 years of age were not in school and had not graduated (U.S. Census, P-20, No. 206). In fact, of those who reach the senior year in high school, girls are somewhat more likely than boys to graduate (U.S. Census, P-20, No. 185).[2] Boys seem to experience greater tension near the end of high school, and one result of this is their greater likelihood to drop out even when they are nearing completion of high school. The greater difficulty boys have throughout school is also reflected in the greater tendency of boys to fall behind, even when they stay in school. For instance, at age 17, when the average youngster is a senior in high school, 28.5 percent of the boys, compared with only 17.1 percent of the girls, are at least one year behind (U.S. Census, P-20, No. 206). This difference by sex will be considered further later in this chapter.

It was suggested in Chapter 5 that strong forces in our society lead lower-class adolescents to drop out of high school at a higher rate than those at higher social levels. There is an extensive body of literature that suggests that drop-out rates do indeed vary by social class.[3] For instance, of all Americans 16 to 24 years of age in 1964 who had dropped out without having completed high school, 35 percent came from families with less than $3,000 annual income and only 4 percent came from families with $10,000 or more annual income. Since families with such incomes constituted about equal proportions of the total population, those from poorer families clearly had a much greater tendency to drop out of school (U.S.

---

[1] In this chapter a number of U.S. government reports are used as bases for the statements made. Many of these are from the U.S. Bureau of the Census *Current Population Reports*, Series P-20, and they will be referred to as noted here and listed under "United States Bureau of the Census" in the list of references.

[2] It is possible, of course, that some of those not in school at any point in time will return at a later date. This might well be the case, for instance, girls who drop out because of pregnancy. It seems likely, however, that more boys than girls complete their high school education after having dropped out, both because of the greater instrumental value of education for the male and because social mechanisms for this purpose are more available to boys than to girls (for example, in the armed services).

[3] Several reviews of this literature are available. See, for instance, Miller, Saleem, and Herrington (1964) and Dentler and Warshauser (1965).

Census, P-20, No. 148). Even if families are simply divided into two categories by the occupation of the head of household, very large differences are found. Using data collected in 1965, from youngsters 16 and 17 years old, Nam, Rhodes, and Herriott (1968) divided their cases into those from white-collar and those from blue-collar families and found a striking difference in dropout rate. Even when they controlled for a number of other variables (race, religion, region, rural-urban residence), they found that youngsters from blue-collar homes were three times more likely than those from white-collar homes to have dropped out of school. The rate was 13.8 percent for blue-collar boys and 13.2 percent for blue-collar girls, compared with 4.2 percent and 3.6 percent for white-collar boys and girls, respectively.[4]

Differences in educational attainment by social class do not cease at departure from high school. About half of all those who graduate from high school go on to college, but the probability of a high school graduate's going to college is strongly related to his social status. Almost two-thirds of the graduates from white-collar families go to college, compared with little more than one-third of those from blue-collar families. The percent varies from 20 percent of graduates from families with less than $3,000 annual income to 87 percent of those from families with more than $15,000 annual income (U.S. Census, P-20, No. 185).[5] It is also true that the lower the class level of the youngster's family, the more likely he is to attend a two-year rather than a four-year college if he goes at all (U.S. Census, P-20, No. 183). Finally, the higher one's social origins, the greater the chances that he will graduate from college once he has entered (Eckland, 1964).

These differences by social class cannot be explained as wholly due to class-related differences in ability. Even holding ability constant, there is a very significant relationship between social class and going to college (Sewell and Shah, 1967). It also seems unlikely that the difference is due wholly to the more limited finances of lower-class people, since even hold-

---

[4] There has been a rapid decrease in the overall dropout rate during the past decade. Comparing 1960 with 1970, the percent of persons 20 to 29 years of age who completed at least four years of high school has increased from 65 percent to 80 percent for whites and from 40 percent to 61 percent for blacks (U.S. Census, P-20, No. 204). Although most of the change has presumably occurred in the lower classes, there is no reason to believe that the class-related differentials discussed here have ceased to exist.

[5] Not surprisingly, the same source reports a strong relationship between going to college and being in the college preparatory program in high school. Of those in the college preparatory program, 78 percent go to college, compared with only 22 percent of those not in that program. There are no known national statistics on the social class origins of those in the various programs, but it seems highly likely that most of those in the college preparatory program are from the higher status levels.

ing income constant, youngsters from white-collar families are more likely to go to college than those from blue-collar families (Folger and Nam, 1967).

The general differences in college attendance and graduation by social class generally hold for both men and women. Women are overall less likely to go to college than men, however. Only about two out of five female high school graduates complete a year of college by the time they are 20 or 21 years of age, compared with about three out of five male high school graduates (U.S. Census, P-20, No. 194). This sex difference in educational attainment is especially apparent in blue-collar families, the difference being very small among white-collar families (Adams and Meidam, 1968).

The overall findings reviewed here thus lend strong support to the proposition that educational attainment is associated with the social level of origin. The lower the social origin, the lower the average level of educational attainment. This is so whether one looks at those who drop out of high school, those who graduate from high school, those who go to college, or those who graduate from college. The differences by sex are not as striking, although fewer women than men continue their education beyond high school.

Becoming a Worker

It is often difficult to specify with confidence when an individual assumes the responsibilities of adult labor force participation. Even after leaving high school, it is not uncommon for an individual to work for some time and then go to college. Others may go to college, drop out for a while to work full time, and then return to college (Eckland, 1964). Occupations are certainly a crucial index of the social placement of individuals in early adulthood. Yet, it is often difficult to determine when a job should be seen as a temporary convenience and when it should be defined as part of the individual's mature position in society. Also, since people do experience career mobility, one may well question the significance of a first job, even a full-time job. If we are to use occupational placement in early adulthood as a basis for discussion, these issues need to be dealt with.

The work of Blau and Duncan (1967) provides the basis for arguing that the individual's first full-time job does provide valuable information about his social placement in early adulthood and that it has long-term implications for the individual. On the basis of the most intensive analysis of such issues carried out to date, Blau and Duncan estimate that about one-eighth of the men they studied returned to some kind of schooling after having assumed full-time employment. Although this is a sizeable proportion of the total, it clearly suggests that such discontinuities are the exception rather than the rule. Also, in spite of the inclusion of such discontinuous cases in their analysis, they found a strong connection overall between the level of a man's first full-time job and the level of job he holds at some later point in his life. The older the man is (the more years that have elapsed between first and current job), the weaker the connection is, but it remains rather strong even for older men.

Thus, although the first job does not in any sense determine the later social placement of the individual, it does provide an accurate indication in most cases of the level at which the individual begins adulthood, and it provides the baseline from which any career mobility must occur.

Not surprisingly, the relationship between level of educational attainment and level of occupation is close, whether one takes the first full-time job or some later job as the point of reference.[6] There is also a rather direct relationship between the level of a person's education and his income. Even while still relatively young (25 to 34 years of age), working men who have four or more years of college earn almost twice as much on the average as do men who never entered high school (U.S. Labor, No. 103).[7] Perhaps even more important, there is a greater tendency for those with less education not to have a job at all. Among young men 16 to 24 years of age in 1968, 10 percent of those who had graduated from high school but were not in college were unemployed compared with 19 percent of those who were high school dropouts (U.S. Labor, No. 108). In general, those who are unemployed, and especially those who lose their jobs, tend to be more poorly educated than those who remain employed (U.S. Labor, No. 106). Thus the lower the individual's level of education, the lower the level of his job, the lower his income, and the more likely he is to lose his job.

One of the important findings in recent research on this subject, however, is that the individual's social background continues to be an important factor in determining his adult social level, even when his level of education has been taken into account. That is, within a group of young men, all of whom have the same level of education, those whose fathers have higher-level occupations will themselves have higher-level occupations

---

[6] In fact, Blau and Duncan found that the relationship is somewhat stronger if a later job is considered. This is an outcome, presumably, of the fact that some people obtain further education after becoming full-time workers. Eckland (1964) found, for instance, that only about one-third of his sample graduated from college within four years after entering but that almost three-fourths did so within ten years after entering.

[7] A number of reports from the U.S. Department of Labor will be referred to in this chapter. They are referred to in the references under United States Department of Labor, *Special Labor Force Report Series.*

(Blau and Duncan, 1967). One reason presumably is that not all the characteristics needed in occupations are specifically taught in school—interpersonal skills and the value of deferring gratifications, for instance. Another is undoubtedly the assistance that highly placed fathers can give their sons, through either useful advice or personal contacts. In any event, although education is extremely important as a means of occupational placement, it is not the only determinant.

The occupational placement of the young man is of central importance in determining the social position of his wife and children, but it is also important to recognize the increasing involvement of women in the labor force, especially young women. There is no simple choice between career and marriage for women, although the combination of marriage and work is not nearly so common for women as for men. About half of all women work, and two out of every five married women 18 to 44 years of age work. Within this age range, the younger women work more frequently than the older ones. Also, the presence of children in the family has a very strong effect on whether a woman works, especially if they are young children. Over half the married women 18 to 44 years of age without pre-school children work, but only about one-fourth of those with pre-school children do so. It is also striking that the higher the married woman's level of education, the more likely she is to work. (This fact is discussed in the next section.) Finally, as with men, both the level of jobs held by married women and their income from working vary widely, depending on their level of education. Women's income levels are consistently lower, however, than those of men with comparable levels of education (U.S. Labor, No. 103; Waldman, 1970).

Marriage and Parenthood

The great majority of young Americans marry and move out of their parental homes soon after they complete their education, though they tend to live with their parents until that time. (Of children under 18 years of age, 85 percent live with both parents, and only 3 percent live with neither.) Few leave the parental home for a continuing independent bachelor life rather than marriage; only about 4 percent of those 20 to 34 years of age live separate from all relatives. Eighty-nine percent of all men and 94 percent of all women marry before the age of 35, half the men marrying by the age of 23 and half the women by the age of 21. Those with higher levels of education are somewhat older on the average when they marry, but the differences are slight for men. More significantly, men with low incomes remain single more often—only 58 percent of men 25 to 34 years old who have incomes under $3,000 are married compared with 93 per-cent of those with incomes over $10,000 (U.S. Census, P-20, No. 198).

A higher level of education encourages the individual to set high stan-dards of living for himself and his family. There is thus an interesting com-bined effect of level of education and level of income on the tendency of men to marry. Not only do more of those with high levels of income marry, but this effect is especially pronounced for men with high levels of educa-tion. For instance, among men 25 to 34 years old with less than a high school education, 69 percent of those with low incomes (under $3,000) marry compared with 95 percent of those with high incomes (over $10,-000); among college graduates in the same age range and with the same income levels, the comparable figures are 47 percent and 90 percent. Thus, the higher the level of education, the greater the effect low income has on the likelihood that a man will marry (U.S. Census, P-20, No. 198).

There is a more clear-cut relationship between level of education and age at marriage for women than for men. During the past decade, half the women who did not finish high school married before the age of 19, whereas the comparable ages for high school graduates and college women were 20 and 22, respectively. Those who go to college are somewhat more likely to remain single up to the age of 35—about 12 percent compared with about 6 percent of the less well educated (U.S. Census, P-20, No. 186).

Not only do less well educated women marry earlier, they are more likely to have a child very soon after marriage. Within a year of marriage, 63 percent of those who do not finish high school have a child, compared with 42 percent of those who graduate from high school or go beyond. In fact, almost one-fourth of women who drop out of high school have a baby *before* marriage, compared with 5 percent of those who graduate from high school or go beyond. Those who have gone to college are least likely of all to have a baby either before marriage or within a year after marriage. This means that the less well educated women are fulfilling the requirements of the maternal role at an earlier age than their better-educated counterparts. Half of all high school dropouts are mothers before the age of 19, half the high school graduates are mothers by 22, and half the women who go to college are mothers by 24 (U.S. Census, P-20, No. 186).

As noted earlier, the presence of a child (especially a pre-school child) in the family has an effect on the mother's employment. Both the educa-tional level of the mother and the income level of the father also influence the mother's working, however. The interplay of these factors is reflected in the data reported in Table 6.1. The effect of the presence of small chil-dren is clearly shown there. It is not surprising that mothers of young children are less likely to work than are other wives, given the child's dependence on other people. Someone must take care of a small child. If

TABLE 6.1
PERCENTAGE OF WIVES WORKING BY WIFE'S EDUCATION,
HUSBAND'S INCOME, AND AGE OF CHILDREN*

Income of Husband and Presence and Age of Children	All Wives	Wife's Years of School		
		High School Dropout	High School Graduate	At Least Some College
All income classes				
No children under 18	41.0	28.9	50.2	54.0
Children under 6	28.5	26.6	29.0	30.1
Husband's income under $3,000				
No children under 18	31.4	23.7	42.8	54.1
Children under 6	33.4	26.0	43.8	43.7
Husband's income $5,000–$6,999				
No children under 18	47.5	36.6	55.6	59.9
Children under 6	35.7	29.5	38.5	43.7
Husband's income over $10,000				
No children under 18	40.8	29.8	42.0	43.0
Children under 6	18.3	18.3	17.4	19.6

*Adapted from U.S. Labor, No. 120, Table 5.

his mother works, other arrangements must be made, and so it is less likely that such a mother will work. One might expect that this effect of the presence of a small child would be more apparent in higher-income families, since they need a second income less. This effect is also reflected in Table 6.1 ("All Wives" column), with no difference in wives' working rates shown at the lowest income level and the maximum difference shown at the highest level.

What is less expected is the way in which the wife's educational level interacts with these basic patterns. At all income levels and whether or not there are young children, women who were high school dropouts are less likely to work. In fact, highly educated women are almost as likely to work when they have small children and their husbands have high incomes (19.6 percent) as are dropouts who do not have small children and whose husbands have low incomes (23.7 percent). There is also a tendency for wives of middle-income men to work more often than wives of low-income men, especially if the wives have low levels of education.

There is a great deal that could be said about these patterns of female employment, but a few observations are particularly significant for our purposes. First and foremost, these data remind us that the young people whose entry into adulthood is being examined here are not only getting married, they are marrying *each other*. Findings relating to men and women separately need to be combined if we are to achieve an adequate view of the process of becoming an adult. "Pairing off," which absorbs so much time and attention during adolescence, leads to the establishment of new nuclear family units, and the pairs who establish these new units are formed largely within the context of educational institutions. This fact is important for an understanding of the characteristics of the pairs that result.

Two closely related persistent findings have been reported regarding the characteristics of young people who marry each other.[8] The first is that marriage partners tend to be people whose residences before marriage were geographically close together. The second is that such partners tend to be similar to each other in a number of socially significant characteristics, the best-documented ones being age, race, religion, and social class. These two findings reflect the obvious fact that at least in a society in which mate selection is determined by the partners themselves, getting married requires that the partners know each other and that they have some basis of mutual attraction. The society generally exhibits residential segregation by race, social class, and (to a lesser extent) religion, and young people tend to be segregated in age-graded educational institutions. Thus, people who are similar in these respects are more likely than others to get to know each other well enough to wish to marry. It is equally true, however, that, even when people with different social characteristics are in the same context, such as a school, there is a tendency for them to be *classified* with and to choose to *associate* with those who are like themselves. The mate selection process thus reflects both opportunity and selectivity. The so-called "field of eligibles" consists of a "field of desirables" within a "field of availables." Young people have greater opportunity to interact with others like themselves than with those who are different, and they generally prefer the former.

This means that, for the most part, people from similar social class origins and similar levels of educational attainment tend to marry each other. In fact, Blau and Duncan (1967) found that young husbands' occupations are as similar to their wives' fathers' occupations as they are to their own fathers' occupations. Neither of these associations is as strong, however, as that between the husbands' and wives' own levels of education. Thus, the well-educated women in Table 6.1 generally have well-educated husbands, and if the wives have low levels of education the husbands tend to be poorly educated also.[9] This provides a basis for a further

---

[8] This paragraph summarizes a large body of literature. For a review of that literature, see Burchinal (1964).

[9] When differences in social class of origin are found between spouses, more frequently the husband's origin is higher than the wife's (Hollingshead, 1950). Since the

understanding of the pattern of maternal employment shown in Table 6.1. Highly educated women are better able to obtain jobs that pay enough to cover the cost of the care of a young child. Thus, if their husbands have low incomes, it "pays" for them to work, even if they have small children. The general similarity of husbands' and wives' educational levels also suggests that it is unusual for a highly educated woman to be married to a low-income husband, and that in such cases, the husband's low income is likely to be a temporary condition. The wife who works while her husband is in medical or law school would be an example. In general, the occupational level of the husband and that of the wife (if she works) are closely related (U.S. Labor, No. 120). Thus, the highly educated woman who works even when she has small children is better able to justify working on economic grounds and, if her husband has a low income, she is more likely to be doing so as a stop-gap.

Social similarity between marriage partners has more than economic significance, however; it has significance for the nature of the marital relationship itself. Men and women from different social levels define the marital relationship differently. Bernard (1964, pp. 687–89) has referred to two marital patterns, one found more frequently among middle-class couples and the other found more frequently among working-class couples. In the "parallel pattern," more common among working-class couples,

> . . . emphasis is on the role aspects of the marriage, and these roles are defined by tradition. . . . If the man is a good provider, not excessive in his sexual demands, sober most of the time, and good to the children, this is about all a woman can reasonably ask. Similarly, if the woman is a good housekeeper and cook, not too nagging, a willing sex partner, and a good mother, this is all a man can really expect. Each lives his or her own life primarily in a male or a female world. . . . [The] essential characteristic is strong emphasis on certain roles and little emphasis on personality interaction. . . . Duty, not spontaneity, is the key word.

In contrast, the "interactional pattern," more commonly found among middle-class couples,

> . . . demands a great deal more involvement in the relationship on the part of the participants. . . . The role qualifications specified in the parallel pattern are taken for granted; . . . they constitute only a minimum;

---

husband's level determines the level of the couple (and their children), it is less threatening to the man to "marry down" than it is to the woman. It is also true that physical beauty is an important factor in a woman's marriage, and lower-status women who are physically attractive are more likely to marry "up" than are less attractive women from similar origins (Elder, 1969). The fact that more men than women go to college also suggests that husbands will tend to be better-educated than wives, especially if the former went to college.

far more is demanded. Companionship, expressions of love, recognition of personality . . . are among the other and characterizing specifications of this pattern.

It is highly likely that the selection of one's mate is based at least in part on the compatibility of the views the two have of the marital relationship.[10] The more traditional definition of male and female roles and of the marital relationship itself in lower-status couples undoubtedly encourages the view that "the wife's place is in the home." It also reduces the possibility of the two spouses' developing a flexible definition of their roles.

The role of educational attainment is important here. The highly educated woman has spent more time in situations in which she is treated very much the same as a man. She has experienced success in the performance of tasks for which men are rewarded (both in school and in the world of work), and she has learned to value the same kinds of activities and to have many of the same interests as men. It is also true that as one progresses through the educational system, especially in college, one is made more aware of the contingent nature of interpersonal relations. Education tends to sensitize one to the learned nature of social roles and to the great potential for personal expression to be found in interaction with others. Education is thus likely to change one's view of *any* social relations, including the marital one. Since highly educated women tend to marry men who have had similar experiences, it is not surprising that they should define the marital relationship differently from their less well-educated peers.[11]

We have thus seen that the poorly educated woman tends to marry earlier and to have children earlier than the woman who is well educated. She usually marries an equally poorly educated man, and their relationship tends to be a rather traditional one with emphasis on the performance of sex-segregated roles. *One* of the outcomes of this is that the poorly educated wife is less likely to contribute to the family income, whether or not she has small children. Since her husband's occupation is not likely to be a high-paying one, this means that differences in average *family* incomes

---

[10] It is necessary to put this statement in such a speculative form because the available data are limited. Bernard points out, for instance, that even in the lower classes there is some evidence that wives prefer the interactional pattern, though their husbands do not. Most of the more detailed studies of mate selection have been made with middle-class subjects, and although those studies show the considerable importance of personality variables in both mate selection and marital adjustment, it is difficult to know how far to generalize such findings. There is some evidence, however, that personality is a less salient element in the marital relationship of lower-status couples (Kerckhoff and Bean, 1970).

[11] Not all the advantages lie on the side of increased education, however. Sensitivity to the significance of interpersonal contingencies does not automatically make the individual skillful in dealing with them. The increased emphasis on introspection and interpersonal analysis can have negative as well as positive outcomes.

of people with different levels of education are greater than the differences in their individual incomes. Ironically, therefore, in those cases in which the wife's income is most needed and where it could provide the greatest percentage increase in the family income, she is least likely to work.

The End of a Cycle and the Beginning of Another

Whichever of the above criteria one uses to define adulthood—leaving school, getting a full-time job, getting married, or becoming a parent—it is clear that some young people in our society enter adulthood at an earlier age than others. The high school dropout not only leaves the formal socialization agency (the school) before his better-educated peers, but is more likely also to assume the adult roles of worker, spouse, and parent at an earlier age. Practically all men ultimately become full-time workers, almost all men and women (over 90 percent) ultimately marry, and the great majority (over 80 percent) of those who marry become parents. Thus, for most people, "entering adulthood" not only represents the end point in the process of their preparation to participate in the society, it also represents the beginning of their activities as socialization agents. It is a period during which one shifts rather abruptly from being a socializee to being a socializer.

The position that has been taken throughout this volume is that all these elements are interrelated. The kind of socialization process one has experienced influences his ability to function in the adult social roles he assumes, and his performance of each of those adult social roles influences his performance of the others. Those who enter adulthood early perform adult roles in a different way from those who enter adulthood later, in part because they have had different kinds of socialization experiences. They have been in school a shorter time, and they have learned different things while they were there. They have been "cooled out" of the educational system and are thus likely to have less respect for (as well as less skill in) intellectual pursuits. Their family relations have tended to be authoritarian and adult-oriented, and they have found their rewards elsewhere—in the youth culture, in doing things with immediate payoff, in early sexual expression. Planning and deferring gratifications has not been encouraged, and it does not seem to work for them. It is not just differences in knowledge and skill that distinguish the poorly educated person, therefore, but a set of values and motives as well.

It is also true, however, that the kinds of adult positions the poorly educated person enters are different from those the better-educated person enters, and the differences are significant for his performance in those positions. The only kind of job he qualifies for is an unskilled or semiskilled one. Such jobs require no particular intellectual effort, but they do require conformity to externally imposed specifications. The worker is told what to do, how to do it, and when to do it. He is neither required nor permitted to use his own judgment, nor is the quality of the interpersonal relations on the job seen as relevant to getting the work done. This kind of "external" view of the social relations on the job is much the same as the definition of the husband-wife relationship. The "parallel" marital relationship just described involves a similar structured definition of the roles of the spouses.

In contrast, those who have gone further in the educational system have had a different set of experiences, and they enter a different set of adult positions. They have prospered, at least relatively speaking, in elementary and high school. Some have been so successful that they have been encouraged to go on to higher levels of education, but even those who have not gone on have developed a different view of intellectual pursuits. They have at least come to view them as a necessary part of goal achievement, even if the goals they sought in school were largely extracurricular. In any event, staying in the system has generally provided them with both a set of useful skills and a channel of access to higher-status jobs. Such higher-status jobs not only require relatively high levels of educational attainment as a criterion of entry, they also require the individual to carry out a different set of tasks in a different way than do lower-prestige jobs. They require more independence, self-direction, and concern for interpersonal relations. Those who assume such occupational positions, therefore, are strongly encouraged to be sensitive to the quality of their relations with those around them. It is not surprising, therefore, that we also find this same kind of emphasis in the "interactional" marital relationship among more highly educated people.

In Chapter 3, considerable attention was given to the different quality of the parent-child relations found at higher and lower social levels. It was suggested there that lower-class parents were more likely to emphasize conformity, to punish the child for what he does rather than for what he intends, and to respond to his behavior in an expressive rather than an explanatory way. Such parents are less concerned with (and less skillful at) taking the role of the other than are middle-class parents. They are less sensitive to either the immediate or the long-range effects of their own behavior on the child. They are more narrow in their view of the relationship, seeing it almost wholly from their own perspective. Chapters 3 and 4 also suggested that this kind of parent-child relationship is likely to lead to the development in the child of a set of characteristics that are poorly suited to the requirements of the school, and such children are likely to be less successful than middle-class children by the school's standards.

We have now come full circle. The present discussion suggests that those who are less successful in school not only have developed the kinds of values and have the kinds of limitations described earlier, but also find themselves in an adult situation that reinforces these. The responsibilities of adulthood are assumed earlier by the people who are least well prepared to shoulder them, and there is little in their adult experience that will provide further preparation. The qualities of the husband-wife relationship are similar to those of the parent-child relationship discussed earlier. Such an external, conformity-based orientation to these most personal of all relationships promises to begin to reproduce the socialization process described in the earlier chapters. Thus, many authors refer to a "vicious circle."

Yet, it is not wholly accurate to refer to the process in this way. Not *all* children who begin life in family settings of this kind develop the characteristics, have the educational experiences, and enter the kinds of adult positions described here. There is a good deal of "slippage" in the system. It is true both that many lower-class children break out of the circle, and that many higher-class children "slide" somewhere along the line. It is somewhat inaccurate to say that all lower-class intergenerational circles are "vicious." It is also inaccurate to say that all higher-class circles are "benign."

The earlier chapters have placed emphasis largely on the factors that lead to intergenerational continuity. Although at many points it has been stressed that there is no perfect relationship between the social class of origin and the class-related processes described, no attempt has been made to specify *how much* deviation there is from such a perfect relationship, and only brief attention has been given to the reasons one could give for deviation when it occurs. One of the reasons for this is that there is a less than adequate empirical basis for dealing with such issues. They deserve discussion, however, even though some of that discussion is speculative. The next chapter attempts to summarize in schematic form the degree to which the general pattern outlined above actually occurs. Some of the reasons for deviations from this pattern are discussed as well.

seven

AN OVERVIEW OF
THE SOCIALIZATION
PROCESS

The organization of the socialization process is basically the same for all children in this country. Children spend the first five years fairly well isolated within a nuclear family in which parents (and usually siblings) are the central figures. Only later do they expand their social experiences at school and within the larger community. In school, they pass in age-graded groups through a series of classrooms, teachers and peers being the most significant sources of influence. During this period, family influences become progressively less immediately effective. At varying ages, young persons leave school and, usually, assume positions in the larger society as workers, marriage partners, and parents.

Although this basic pattern is the same throughout the society, the emphasis here has been on the variations in the *kinds* of experiences different children have with the several kinds of socialization agents—parents, teachers, peers. The young person plays an active role in this process; he can choose to some extent which of these others he will associate with. Earlier socialization has its most significant effects on the responses of the young person to later experiences. His responses, in turn, influence the view others have of him, and their further response to him will be based on that view. Socialization is thus an interactive or "growth" process, in that earlier events influence the characteristics of the maturing person, the ways in which he behaves, and the nature of his effective social environment. There are continual influences on the individual, and also continual feedback from him to the significant others around him.

Variation among individuals in this growth process could be examined in terms of many kinds of differences: male-female, black-white, Protestant-Catholic-Jew, and so forth. Here, though, we focus on differences by social class. The earlier chapters have sketched the outlines of this variation. At each stage in the process, differences by social class have been noted both in the actions of the socialization agents and in the characteristics and behavior of the maturing individual.

If one looks back over the material in the earlier chapters, it is apparent that it is much easier in the early years of the individual's life to view the socializer-socializee relationship as unidirectional: socializers behave in ways that have certain effects on the socializee. Although there is mutual influence even in the early stages, the influence is much more one-sided than in the later stages. By the time the individual reaches secondary school, the balance is very different. What he does and has done influences the process at least as much as what others do to him. More options are available, and he is both permitted and able to choose among them. As a result, as we shift our attention from the early to the later stages in the process, two changes are apparent. First, we find a shift from a discussion of the *kinds of people* the socializers (especially parents) are to an emphasis on the kinds of *opportunities* for influence the socializers (especially teachers and peers) provide. Second, we find that discussions of the individual shift from a delineation of the kinds of *characteristics* he has developed (what kind of person he is or what he is capable of doing) to descriptions of his *actions* (what he chooses to do).

The central theme of the earlier chapters has been that socialization experiences vary by social class, that these experiences lead to the development of different characteristics in children from different social classes, and that these differences in the children influence both others' treatment of them and the pattern of their own chosen activities, ultimately leading them to assume different adult positions. The earlier socialization outcomes thus influence both the opportunity structure and the choice patterns of children in different social classes; the outcome reflects both what they want and what is open to them. Opportunities at any point in time are a function of the individual's characteristics and past performances (among other things), and the older the child gets the more this is so. Thus, although socialization agencies may be viewed more as sources of opportunity than direct control as the child matures, what opportunities they provide will vary. And although the child becomes progressively more determinative of his own socialization experiences, the number of options open to him will depend heavily on what he has done in the past. His choices from among available opportunities will also depend on the outcomes of previous experience, both because of what he has learned to value and because of what he has learned is possible.

We have thus seen how the socialization process varies by social class, and this variation would lead us to expect a great deal of continuity in social class placement from one generation to the next. It has been shown that middle-class parents generally rear their children in such a way that they develop greater self-control, a stronger achievement orientation, greater sensitivity to others, and a more complex linguistic and cognitive structure, than lower-class children show. Such characteristics are well suited to the expectations of the school, and middle-class children thus tend to be more successful in school from the beginning. This initial advantage tends to snowball, so that an increasing gap occurs between those who are initially more and less successful. Not only does this differential in academic performance feed upon itself, but those who are less successful tend to withdraw from intellectual pursuits and "success-oriented" activities, becoming more involved in adolescence in the youth culture and in various antiestablishment activities. The school, in turn, adjusts its opportunity structure to the past performance of the child, the more academically successful being rewarded by both positive sanctions and increased opportunities. Those who are less successful in school thus tend to leave the system earlier and enter into adult positions earlier. The fact that they are not well prepared for many adult occupational positions means that they are likely to enter low-status positions, and the fact that they marry and have children at a relatively early age means that they are unlikely later to obtain the credentials necessary for higher-status positions. The academically more successful student tends to stay in the educational system longer (delaying marriage and parenthood while doing so), thereby obtaining the necessary credentials for higher-status occupations. Thus, those who start life at higher status levels seem to be destined to remain there, and those who start life at lower levels seem unlikely to rise in the system.

Yet we know that mobility does occur. In fact, one of the major characteristics of the American social system as discussed in Chapter 1 is the fact that mobility not only is highly valued and facilitated but frequently occurs. How can we reconcile the existence of mobility and the social emphasis on mobility with the evidence provided in the last four chapters? Is it reasonable to argue that the socialization process varies by one's social class of origin and that socialization affects one's social class of destination and still acknowledge the existence of significant amounts of social mobility? The answer is "Yes," but in order to give that answer it is necessary to keep in mind that the associations between social class and socialization processes and outcomes that we have examined earlier are less than perfect. Throughout the earlier discussion it has been necessary to say, "There is a good deal of variation," or, "In general, this is true." The characteristics of the socialization process and outcome do vary by social class, but one cannot predict the process or outcome perfectly from a knowledge of an individual's social class position.

This leads to a concern with a number of further questions: If the patterns described earlier are *generally* found, how general are they? How *much* relationship is there between social class and socialization? If the relationship is not perfect, what is the nature of the association that does exist? If it is not a simple case of "cause and effect," what *is* the role of social class in the socialization process? Without turning to the infinite variety of individual differences, is there any basis for understanding the patterns of mobility that do occur? Is an understanding of the role of social class in the socialization process helpful in explaining mobility as well as continuity? The rest of this chapter is devoted to a consideration of such questions.

Evidence for a Class-Based Model of Socialization

The previous chapters have presented the basis for saying that socialization varies by social class throughout three periods of the child's life: the pre-school, elementary school, and secondary school years. When one turns to the issue of the adequacy of the evidence for making general statements about such matters, two things become very apparent. First, the evidence is more adequate for late than for early childhood. Most of the studies of pre-school children, for instance, used relatively small samples which cannot be assumed to be representative of the total population. Second, it is easier to find evidence of the *outcome* of the socialization process than it is to find evidence about the process itself. We have more adequate information about how children from different social classes differ at various ages than we do about the differences in their experiences. We know, for instance, that lower-class children perform progressively less adequately in school in the early years, and we assume that their performance is the result of different school experiences, but we do not have extensive direct evidence about those experiences. Thus, it will be necessary at some points in this discussion to make certain assumptions about what *would* be found if we had better data.

Our general problem is to describe how much relationship there is between social class and socialization, but socialization involves a whole series of events and outcomes. Thus, it will be necessary to examine the relationship between social class as a variable and a number of other variables that represent measures of socialization events and outcomes. The question of *how much* relationship there is requires a measure of association between social class and each of these other variables. The most common measure used in the social sciences, and the one to be used here, is the correlation coefficient (*r*). The degree of the relationship between social class and socialization can be represented, therefore, by a series of correlation coefficients.[1]

TABLE 7.1
CORRELATIONS BETWEEN SOCIAL LEVEL OF ORIGIN
AND SOCIALIZATION VARIABLES

Socialization Variable	*r**	*Class Measure*†	*Source*‡
Pre-School			
Parental values (self-direction vs. conformity)	.37	SES	K
Father's intelligence	.29	SES	D
Number of siblings	−.28	Occ	D
Nursery school or kindergarten experience	.37	Ed	C
Elementary School (Grade 6, except first item)			
Verbal ability, grade 1	.24	Ed	C
Verbal ability	.31	Ed	C
Average verbal ability of classmates	.32	Ed	C
% of classmates whose mothers went to college	.43	Ed	C
Son's perception of parental educational encouragement	.21	SES	F
Perception of parental interest	.17	Ed	C
Favorableness of self-concept	.18	Ed	C
Sense of control of environment	.19	Ed	C
Son's educational expectations	.36	SES	F
Son's occupational expectations	.25	SES	F
Son's grades in school	.38	SES	F
Ninth Grade			
Verbal ability	.35	Ed	C
Average verbal ability of classmates	.29	Ed	C
% of classmates whose mothers went to college	.35	Ed	C

[1] Correlation coefficients range from −1.00 to +1.00. A positive coefficient indicates that as one variable gets larger, the other does also; a negative coefficient indicates that as one gets larger, the other gets smaller. A coefficient of 1.00 would mean that all the variation in one variable (say, educational attainment) could be understood or explained by knowledge of the individuals' scores on another variable (say, a social class index). From the knowledge of the second variable, you could predict precisely any individual's score on the first variable. On the other hand, a coefficient of .00 would mean that knowledge of the individuals' scores on the second variable would not tell us anything about their scores on the first. The larger the correlation coefficient, therefore, the stronger the relationship between the two variables.

TABLE 7.1 (Contd.)

Socialization Variable	r*	Class Measure†	Source‡
Ninth Grade (Contd.)			
Son's perception of Parental educational encouragement	.45	SES	F
Perception of parental Interest	.21	Ed	C
Sense of control of Environment	.21	Ed	C
Son's educational expectations	.41	Occ	R
Son's occupational expectations	.41	SES	F
Son's grades in school	.51	SES	F
Twelfth Grade			
Verbal ability	.33	Ed	C
Average verbal ability of classmates	.29	Ed	C
% of classmates in college preparatory course	.29	Ed	C
Son's perception of parental educational encouragement	.42	SES	S
Perception of parental interest	.20	Ed	C
Favorableness of self-concept	.20	Ed	C
Sense of control of environment	.18	Ed	C
Son's educational aspirations	.38	SES	S
Daughter's desired education for her husband	.38	SES	T
Son's occupational aspirations	.37	SES	S
Daughter's desired occupation for her husband	.37	SES	T
Son's grades in school	.28	SES	F
Social status of son's best friends	.27	SES	D
Early Maturity			
Son's educational attainment	.40	Ed	D
Daughter's age at first marriage	.17	SES	B
Son's age at first job	.34	Ed	D
Prestige Level of son's first job	.32	Ed	D
Number of children born (wives 22-26 years old)	−.20	Occ	D

* Many of these correlation coefficients are based on white samples rather than upon a representative sample of the total population. Although the coefficients for non-whites are often quite different from those for whites, the fact that whites constitute the very great majority of the total population suggests that coefficients for a combined sample of whites and nonwhites would not be much different from those presented here.

† Several different measures of social class position are used in the several studies from which these results come. They are, in general, of three types: (1) A measure of the level of the occupation of the father (Occ.); (2) A measure of the level of educational attainment of the father (Ed.); (3) An index made up of several variables, including father's occupation and education, but also sometimes including other variables (SES).

‡ The letters in this column refer to the sources of the correlations reported. The sources to which the letters refer are: (K) Kohn, 1969; (D) One of the following publications by Duncan (Blau and Duncan, 1967; Duncan, 1968; Duncan, Haller, and Portes, 1968); (C) Coleman, Campbell, et al., 1966; (F) Unpublished data collected by the author in Fort Wayne, Indiana; (R) Rehberg, Sinclair, and Schafer, 1970; (S) Either of the following publications by Sewell (Sewell and Shah, 1968; Sewell, Haller, and Ohlendorf, 1970); (T) Turner, 1964; (B) Bayer, 1969.

Only relationships for which there are good empirical bases will be considered. A number of these are presented in Table 7.1 in the order of their relevance during the chronological periods discussed in the previous chapters. The coefficients reported there are based either on very large national samples, on large and diverse urban or state samples, or on the author's own somewhat more restricted sample, which has been carefully compared with those larger ones. Thus, although the size of a coefficient should not be taken as wholly precise and unchanging, there is good reason to see these coefficients as at least good approximations of the true relationships.

It is clear that social class, measured in a variety of ways, is significantly related to a number of socialization variables. The characteristics of parents, the abilities of children (of all ages), the nature of the parent-child relationship, the academic performance of children, the children's aspirations, their social relations, and their ultimate educational and occupational attainment—all of these vary by social class. The great majority of the coefficients are in the range from .20 to .40, however, which is not very high. Thus, although social class seems to be an important variable throughout the socialization process, it can explain only a rather limited amount of the variation in the process and the outcome.

Perhaps even more interesting than the absolute size of these coefficients is the fact that they are of about the same size at all points in the process. In fact, the relationship between the parents' social status and their *own* characteristics is basically the same as the relationship between parental social status (our measure of social class of origin) and the *child's* characteristics, including his adult social status. These relationships are, in turn, basically the same as the relationship between parental social status and the various socialization variables during childhood. Thus, social class of origin seems to have a modest but quite pervasive relevance throughout the period being studied here. Although we have seen some evidence of a "cumulative deficit" during the school years, the data reported in Table 7.1 do not support the notion of an overall cumulative effect of social class of origin. Social class seems to have an unmistakable effect on the socialization process and its outcome, but this effect is not progressively larger as the child matures.[2]

The Role of Social Class in Socialization

A basic problem posed by these findings and by those more detailed

---

[2] Blau and Duncan (1967) have very persuasively made this same point. They argue that a cumulative effect is more demonstrable in the case of racial identity, Negroes being disadvantaged at all points in the process, regardless of their position at an earlier point. This matter is referred to again in the Appendix.

findings reviewed earlier in this volume is to provide an idea of the place of social class in the socialization process. Certainly social class of origin does not in any direct way "cause" the socialization process. Nevertheless, it is evidently a factor that must be dealt with if we are to understand that process. A view of the role of social class in socialization has been implicit throughout the earlier discussion, but it may be valuable to make it quite explicit here and to attempt a summary statement of it.

Socialization has been described as a process in which the socializee interacts with socializers in such a way that he acquires skills, knowledge, values, and motives that are functional in his later performance of adult roles. In the course of the process, the socializee becomes increasingly instrumental in determining the degree and nature of his interaction with the socializers. Such a view puts heavy emphasis on social interaction, and it suggests two rather different ways in which the level of one's social origins may be significant in the study of socialization.

(1) SOCIAL CLASS AS A CONTEXT.   Here the focus is on the kinds of people encountered by those in different social classes. Since the residential pattern in our society separates classes to a high degree, and since in any event a child's early years are generally spent within the close confines of a nuclear family, the kinds of people young children encounter will vary to the extent that adults at different social levels have different character-istics. As Chapter 3 suggested, and as Table 7.1 also reflects, lower-status parents tend to have different characteristics from higher-status parents. This difference in social context goes beyond the nuclear family, however. Table 7.1 also shows that children from higher social class levels are more likely to go to nursery school and kindergarten, to have more intelligent classmates, to have classmates whose mothers have more education, and (in high school) to have more classmates who are in college preparatory courses. Whatever the characteristics of the individual children, therefore, those from different social levels are placed in different social contexts.

(2) SOCIAL CLASS AS A BASIS OF EXPECTATIONS.   As just suggested, people in different positions in the social structure may behave differently when placed in the same situation. For instance, lower-class parents tend to respond differently from middle-class parents to their children's mis-behavior. In short, the behavior of actors varies according to their social characteristics. It is equally true, however, that the behavior of actors varies according to the social characteristics of the person toward whom their behavior is directed. Girls are generally treated differently from boys. Our behavior toward old people is different from our behavior toward children. In fact, such factors as age and sex constitute significant social categories both because we vary our behavior according to the age and sex of the other person and because we expect different behavior according to the

age and sex of the other. Social class is also a significant social category. We both behave differently toward people according to their social class level and expect different kinds of behavior from them, according to class. Thus, teachers, counselors, peers—even parents—are likely to respond to a child not simply as a *child,* but as a child in a specific social position. Teachers may expect that lower-class students will do poorly and thus fail to take any corrective action if they do. Counselors may encourage a middle-class high school senior to go to college irrespective of his academic record. A parent may warn a child not to have too high aspirations because he comes from a poor family.

It is not always easy to separate the effects of these two kinds of influences—the influence of contexts and the influence of differential expectations. Yet the distinction is an important one to make, since it has implications both for an understanding of the socialization process and for any proposed attempts to alter that process. For instance, if lower-class children are "permitted" to enter contexts that have previously been wholly middle class but are responded to differently because they are lower class, one cannot expect the outcome to be the same as for middle-class children. In such a case, however, much will depend on another element, namely, what the child *does.* Contexts and expectations constitute a matrix of social influences, but the child is an active, not a passive, participant in the socialization process. To some extent, he can move within his social context, and he can meet or deviate from the expectations others have of him. Socialization outcomes are thus not easily predicted directly from a knowledge of class-related contexts and expectations.

The view of the role of social class in socialization being developed here suggests that there is an interplay between the formative experiences of the child, what others expect of him, and what he becomes. The latter not only is an *ultimate* outcome but is an active element in the process from the beginning. What the child becomes is not a simple function of what people expect him to be. Although expectations are important influences on the self-other experiences of the child, and although those expectations are influenced by his social class position, his behavior at one point in time will also influence what is expected of him at a future point. Similarly, although the social context in which a child is reared is a potent influence on the kinds of experience he will have, he becomes increasingly able to select from within that context those experiences which he finds rewarding. Outcomes thus influence contexts and expectations as well as the reverse.

This suggests that as the child gets older there is an increasing tendency for earlier outcomes to influence later outcomes. To the extent that he can choose experiences from within his social context (or even change contexts), and to the extent that others' expectations become adjusted to his previous performances, what he will do in the future becomes increasingly predictable from what he has done in the past. Although one may view him as more free to choose his later socialization experiences, *what* he chooses will increasingly be a function of his previous behavior. Another important determiner of his future choices will be his opportunities for choice. Those opportunities will be limited in part by the context, and in part they will be limited by various "gatekeepers" (for example, college admissions officers) who estimate the likelihood of future performance from knowledge of past performances. Thus, it is not only increasingly unlikely that the individual will choose to change the pattern of his performances, it is also less likely that he will be permitted to do so.

Such a view leads to the suggestion that the role of social class in the socialization process changes during the individual's lifetime. It begins as a significant determiner of the social context within which the child is reared. As he grows older and moves into a broader social context, his class of origin serves as a point of reference in the responses others make to him, and to the extent this is so, it also serves as a point of reference in his view of himself. His behavior, however, provides a basis for the constant reassessment of this class-based expectation both by others and by himself. To the extent that it is consistent with the original expectation, it "confirms" and reinforces that expectation. On the other hand, to the extent that it deviates from that expectation, it may lead either to pressures toward conformity with the expectation or to alteration of the expectation. Although the social context may continue to be somewhat different for people from different origins, this interplay between expectations and performances becomes an increasingly important part of the process. The association between origin and outcome, therefore, cannot be understood without reference both to contexts and to this interplay between expectations and performances, and the relative significance of these two sources of influence shifts as the child matures.

This view provides the basis for a general model of socialization that includes social class as a variable. It also points up several possible bases of discontinuity from generation to generation. A description of such a model and a discussion of sources of discontinuity are the concern of the following two sections.

A Class-Based Model of Socialization

If social class serves both as a determiner of context and as a basis for expectations, one ought to be able to predict something about the outcome of the socialization process from a knowledge of the social class of origin of the individual. As Table 7.1 suggests, context, performances, expectations, and outcomes are all somewhat predictable from social class of origin. If the process is as the earlier discussion has outlined, however, the connection between origin and outcome can be understood only by reference to both context and the interplay between performances and expectations. Initial performances outside the family certainly reflect the influence of the child's early social context, but they also occur in a setting in which the significant others have some basis for expectations of his performance. These expectations will, at least in part, be based on conceptions of a connection between social class and levels of performance. Children whose performance deviates from what is expected present a problem to their significant others. What these others will do about such deviations, however, is problematic. Some may alter their expectations, but others may persist in their expectations and use various means to influence the child to behave in accordance with them.

Since the set of potentially significant others available to the child both within and outside the family is rather large, he may receive varied responses to his performances from different sources. Because some of them will have more general significance in his life than others, he will learn to attend to some of these sources of response more than to others. At the same time, their general significance to him will in part be a function of how favorably they respond. The child thus moves within a complex network of relationships in which there is not only variation in response but also the potential for him to alter the degree to which he attends to these responses. The interplay between performances and expectations is thus extremely complex in its effects on the child.

Children's differences in ability when they enter school need to be considered here as well. If we focus our attention on the child's experience in school and on the kinds of performance generally rewarded there, it is important to recognize that children do seem to enter school with varying levels of ability. In fact, the general expectation that lower-class children will perform less well is at least in part based on evidence of such differences. It is a highly controversial matter as to whether such differences in ability should be viewed as "given," in the sense that they are inborn, or whether they should be viewed as the result of the child's pre-school experience, or both. Chapter 3 reviewed material that strongly suggests that the ability to perform school tasks is heavily influenced by the child's pre-school experience, but such evidence does not prove that there are no biologically determined ability differences associated with social class. It will not be possible to resolve this issue here nor even to present the complex nature of the problem. For present purposes, however, it will be sufficient simply to note that from the perspective of the school at least, these differences *are* given, and that ability levels vary by social class from the beginning. In the model being presented, therefore, they are seen as a function of the context from which the child comes. If the reader prefers to view this as a biological *as well as* a social context, it will not alter the model appreciably. The model does assume, however, that the variation in ability is in large part due to social influences and not just biological differences.

If we conceive of ability and social class of origin as combined (and not wholly separable) sources of determination of the child's early performance level, and if significant others respond to that early performance, later performance can be viewed as a function of the response to the early performance. In the same manner, later performances will continue to receive response, and such repeated patterns of performance and response will tend to stabilize. Performance level will become relatively consistent, and an increasingly clear set of expectations of performance will develop, not only in the eyes of the significant others, but in the child's own eyes. Such self-expectations establish a basis for his view of the future, his level of aspiration.

A basic conceptual problem here is the extent to which this should be seen as a simple linear process. Can we, for instance, say that something like the following statement adequately summarizes the process: Class of origin and ability→Early performance→Others' response→Later performance→Others' response→Stability of performance→Clarity of expectations→Child's aspirations→Level of attainment? What such a linear statement suggests is that once we have taken early performance into account, the child's social origin and ability level do not affect either the others' response or his later performance. This seems clearly unacceptable if the ideas of class context and class-related expectations and response are to be included in the model. Yet it seems equally clear that the direct influence of origins diminishes during the process.

No simple diagrammatic presentation can adequately reflect the interactive nature of the process conceived of here, but Figure 7.1 is a simplified version and can form the basis of a discussion of the conceptual issues involved. It is basically a longitudinal model in which the factors at each point in the process are linked with earlier and later ones. The links, represented by arrows in the figure, reflect a flow of influence. The presence of an arrow suggests a significant source of direct influence on the factor named, and where arrows are not present, the connection between the two factors is viewed as indirect. For instance, early performance is shown as directly influenced by the child's ability and social origins, but the response to the performance is influenced by both the performance itself and his background. His later performance, in turn, is influenced by both his earlier performance and by the response others made to that earlier performance. No *direct* effect of his background is shown here after the first two steps, but since early performance and others' response were both influenced by

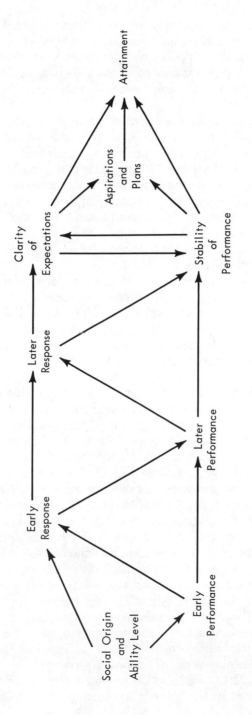

FIGURE 7.1

Schematic Diagram of Flow of Influences

his background, and since they in turn influence later developments, his background has an *indirect* influence on the later developments. The model also suggests that stable performance and a set of stable expectations (his own and others') evolve together and mutually influence each other. They, in turn, affect his level of aspiration, which influences his level of attainment.

Such a diagram reflects some of the important characteristics of the model being developed here, but not all. It reflects the importance of social class as an early context that influences the child's ability to perform those tasks presented by the school. It also reflects the important influence his background may have on the evaluations others make of his performances. More generally, it emphasizes the interplay between the individual's behavior and the responses others make to that behavior. Finally, it suggests the decreasing direct effect of origins, the continuing effect of social response, and the increasing importance of stable patterns (both behavioral and perceptual) within the individual.

Three important aspects of the model are not represented in the diagram, however. First, the diagram does not suggest the continuing significance of the context within which the child lives. Social class as context is significant not only within the nuclear family, but also within the neighborhood, the relatively class-homogeneous elementary school, and the relatively class-heterogeneous secondary school. If elementary school teachers are of a different type (or quality) in schools in various neighborhoods, or if the child goes to school with others who are all of the same class as he is (or, rarely, of a different class), context continues to be very significant. Second, the diagram does not suggest the diversity of potentially significant others. The earlier chapters have used the three reference points of family, peers, and school officials as reminders of that diversity. But even within each of these (though less so in the family) there is diversity, and the child is likely to receive somewhat different responses from different peers and from different teachers. This diversity, together with his increasing ability to choose from among these varying sources of response, means that no simple representation of the response of others adequately reflects the complexity of the process. Finally, the diagram suggests that others' evaluations influence the individual to perform differently and to develop a general level of aspiration, but it does not indicate the degree to which these responses of others may also limit his *opportunities* for performance. To the extent that teachers and others act as "gatekeepers," they not only evaluate, they also structure the individual's options. Level of aspiration and plans for the future involve not only an image of how well one can perform but also a view of the opportunity structure.

Thus, the model of socialization proposed here is one that is based on the significance of social structure and interaction, and social class affects both. The nucleation of the family and the residential segregation of social classes place the child in a reasonably homogeneous social context throughout his childhood. Early socialization in such class-homogeneous contexts differentially prepares children for school experiences. These experiences and the social contexts within which they occur also tend to be somewhat class-specific, but probably less so than his pre-school experiences. The patterns of interaction he engages in with significant others both at home and in school will reflect not only the basic characteristics of these others but also their view of the class system and his place in it. Their responses to him will influence not only his later performances but also his relationship with them, leading him to become differentially attentive to responses from different sources. His performances in turn will influence not only the expectations he and the others have of his future performances, but also the opportunities open to him and the choices he makes from among them. Throughout, his and the others' view of his place in the social class system as well as the class-related characteristics of the setting may well color the process, but increasingly the effects of his class of origin become indirect rather than direct. They remain relevant only to the extent that his behavior "confirms" class-related expectations. A stable pattern of self-other relations and performance-expectation levels develops that is relatively self-perpetuating and increasingly resistant to either social contextual or interpersonal influences. Although we would not want to say that he is "fully socialized," the characteristics he develops during the early phases of the process do have a continuing effect on what happens later.

Sources of Variation

Such a model of socialization does not, of course, require that there be intergenerational continuity. There are within it numerous potential sources of influence that can lead to deviation from any such direct links between the social position of the parents and that of the child as an adult. Although the emphasis in the previous section (and throughout the book) has been on the factors that would tend to lead to continuity, continuity is only part of the picture. The aim in this section is to sketch in some of the rest of it. No attempt will be made to be comprehensive in doing so, however. Instead, a brief review of some of the sources of deviation from class-related consistency in context and expectations is offered, which refers back to the general process outlined in the previous section.

A basic assumption of the model is that the pre-school contexts of children vary by social class and are relatively homogeneous. Although this is generally the case, it is not wholly true. Not all families live in class-homogeneous neighborhoods, for instance, although most do. Even within the family, parents need not have the same social class backgrounds, although the tendency to marry someone of a similar background is strong. At the pre-school level, the significance of social class is largely its association with different patterns of parent-child relations. This variation is generally seen as a function of the parents' experiences in the larger society, especially their educational and occupational experiences. Although there is a relationship between educational level and occupational position on the one hand and child-rearing values on the other, the association is far from perfect (Kohn, 1969). It is also true that within any social class level, the mother's as well as the father's work experience seems to be a significant source of variation in parental values (Kohn, 1959). Finally, the degree to which parents are satisfied with their social position will also affect the ways parents at any social level will attempt to influence their children (Kahl, 1953). Thus, there is considerable variation within the contexts experienced by pre-school children in any given class.

Presumably as a result of such variation, not all children within a single class develop the same characteristics, nor are they the same in school-relevant abilities when they get to school. There is undoubtedly some validity in the statement that teachers respond to children's performances in part according to their view of what is "normal" for children from various social levels (Rosenthal and Jacobson, 1968), but such categorical expectations must also contend with variations in the actual behavior of the children. It may also be that peer influence is stronger when it comes from those of similar background, and thus it tends to reinforce class-related characteristics (Alexander and Campbell, 1964), but not all children from a given social level will be equally responsive to such influences. Even those studies that lend support to these expectations of class-related responses from significant others also show that some teachers respond more fully than others in accord with the child's performance rather than his class and that many children seem to be strongly influenced by peers from different social backgrounds. In any event, schools vary widely in the kinds of teachers and peers the child encounters. Finally, even in high school, it can be shown that the lack of homogeneity of families within a social class makes a difference in the child's plans and aspirations (Krauss, 1964). Working-class youngsters who have mothers in white-collar jobs or whose mothers came from higher social class origins than their fathers have higher aspirations than others from the same class.

Such considerations suggest that many combinations of sources of influence may be experienced by children who begin their lives at any given level in the stratification system. No analysis such as that presented here can hope to deal with all these possible combinations, but it seems certain that they exist. Children similarly placed in the stratification system will have varied experiences, which will result from differences among their parents, differences in the neighborhoods they live in, and differences in the structure of the educational systems they move through. Not only their social contexts, but the degree to which class of origin influences the experiences they have *within* those social contexts, varies. Although there seems to be some tendency for the combinations of influences to be different at different class levels, considerable variation clearly occurs at each level.

Conclusion

The previous two sections have had rather different emphases. The first stressed the role of social class in the socialization process, although it sought to show how the effects of social class of origin become increasingly indirect as the child grows older. The second considered a few of the bases of variation in the association between social class of origin and socialization. Both of these emphases are needed. There is no question that social class is a significant factor in socialization, but there is equally sound basis for emphasizing the sources of variation in the role social class plays in the process.

To emphasize such sources of variation is not to argue that class-related factors are not important so much as it is to suggest that many of these factors are experienced in varying degrees by children from similar social levels. No measure of level of origin can be expected to summarize the correlates of social class that are significant in the socialization process, whether it is a measure of occupational prestige, educational attainment, or some more complex index. This is true even when the focus of attention is the nuclear family. When one broadens the range of class-related variables to a consideration of such matters as neighborhood and school characteristics, the variation becomes even greater.

Within the study of socialization, therefore, social class is a convenient global index that summarizes a number of highly relevant factors but does not fully represent any of them. Social class is an important focus of attention in the study of the socialization process because a number of significant characteristics of the process tend to vary according to the level of origin of the individual. It is these characteristics, rather than social class as such, that affect the outcome. It has been suggested that socialization outcomes depend on how one's significant others behave and on what these others expect of the socializee. Children who begin life at different levels in the stratification system tend to encounter different kinds of significant others, people who behave in different ways. Social class is also important because it is one of the sets of categories people in our society use in classifying each other and in determining what kinds of behavior are appropriate in relation to each other. Thus, both the social context and the expectation of others experienced by children tend to vary by their level of origin.

Given the many ways in which social class of origin influences the socialization process, it may seem remarkable that the amount of intergenerational continuity is not greater than it is. The considerable amount of mobility that occurs is often viewed as an indication that the society is indeed an "open" one and that the channels and mechanisms of achievement are freely accessible. The noncumulative nature of the effect of social class suggests that there is a constant counter force at work. On the other hand, if we recognize that mobility simply refers to the absolute difference in the level of the occupation of a father and his son, the fact of mobility takes on somewhat different meaning. If it should happen, for instance, that *all* sons had occupational positions a certain social distance higher than their fathers, then *everyone* would be upwardly mobile but *no one* would change his relative position in the stratification system. To some extent, that is what has been happening during the past few decades. The overall pattern of the occupational structure has shifted upward, so that there are many more high-prestige jobs today than formerly. Thus, a significant part of the intergenerational mobility people have experienced has been due to the increased demands for workers in such higher-status jobs.

Although upward mobility is experienced by some people from all levels of origin, there seem to be some limits on the degree of mobility that is likely. For instance, the intergenerational move from a blue-collar to a white-collar job appears to be more difficult to make than a move of equal distance within either the blue- or the white-collar categories. Perhaps even more significant for our purposes, downward mobility across the white-collar–blue-collar line is much less common than downward movement within either of the two categories. This seems to mean, then, that upward mobility into the white-collar category is difficult, but once a family has "made it" into that category, it is not very likely to drop below it again (Blau and Duncan, 1967).

In spite of these limitations on the fluidity of mobility in the United States, Blau and Duncan provide evidence that there has been a greater amount of upward mobility in this country than in any of the other Western nations. In particular, there seems to be a greater opportunity in this country for those from working-class backgrounds to achieve the highest-prestige occupations. Whether such a degree of openness is continuing is at least debatable, however. For instance, Spady (1967) provides evidence that although the overall level of educational attainment has gone up dramatically in the United States in the past forty years, there has been an increase in the degree to which one's origin influences one's level of attainment. It is possible, therefore, that even a high overall level of upward mobility can be associated with decreasing openness in the system.

Such observations raise a fundamental question about the meaning of "opportunity" in this society. Turner (1964) has suggested that one may look at the achievement process as either a "race" or a "ladder." In the former case, one's view calls for all those involved to be able to start from the same point and to have an equal chance to go as far as they can from that point. The view of achievement as a "ladder" suggests that people begin the process at different levels, and the view of opportunity calls for them to be able to go as far as they can from the point of their origin. If we recognize that individuals do, in fact, begin life at different levels, and if the ideal conception of achievement we hold is one of a "race" rather than a "ladder," clearly something must be done to bring everyone to the same starting point.

On the other hand, the view of the role of social class in the socialization process that has been presented in this volume makes it clear that more than a "starting point" is involved. The effects of one's origin are felt throughout the process. Various sources of influence are experienced during the "race," which alter the individual's chances. Any attempt to equalize the opportunity structure in the direction of a wholly equal "race," therefore, must consider the total process and not just its beginnings.

The purpose of this volume, however, is not to demonstrate the degree to which this is or is not an open society nor to argue that it should be more or less open than it is. The purpose is to review the ways in which one's point of origin in one part of the social structure (the stratification system) influences the process by which one reaches his adult destination in that same structure. If that task has been adequately carried out, the bases of both continuity and mobility have been somewhat illuminated. The basic belief that underlies the volume is that such illumination is a necessary prerequisite for any evaluation of the present situation and for any proposals for its alteration.

ON BEING BLACK

In the body of this report an attempt has been made to describe variations in the socialization process and outcome that can be attributed to differences in point of origin in the stratification system. One of the issues raised by that discussion is its implication for notions of "equality of opportunity" in the United States. Most discussions of equality of opportunity are even more concerned with the significance of racial identity than of class origin, and it can be argued that race is a much more important factor than class in limiting an individual's opportunities. This Appendix discusses briefly some of the factors that need to be taken into account if the variable of race is to be viewed in the light of the earlier analysis of the role of class in the socialization process.

The Association of Race and Class

The great majority (about 88 percent) of the American population is classified as white, and the nonwhite population is very largely (about 92 percent) Negro. For our purposes, therefore, it is possible to concentrate on a comparison of two categories, whites and blacks.[1] The most basic question to be raised here is the degree to which racial identity is associated with position in the stratification system. The answer, clearly, is that there is a very close association. Blacks are concentrated much more in the lower levels than are whites. For instance, 71 percent of all white heads of households under 45 years of age have completed high school, and 17 percent of them have completed four years of college; the comparable figures for blacks are 43 percent and 4 percent. The average income of white families in 1965 was $7,498 if the head of the family was male and $4,101 if the head was female; for blacks the figures were $4,593 and $2,464. About one-fourth of all white heads of households are employed in the two highest-prestige occupation groups, but less than one-tenth of black heads of households are found in those occupations. (U.S. Census, P-20, Nos. 168 and 200).

Such massive differences in the class distributions of the two populations cannot be ignored when comparisons are made for other purposes. If there are differences in the socialization process and outcomes according to position in the stratification system, as the body of this report has demonstrated, any comparison between blacks and whites would be expected to reflect those class differences. It is possible, therefore, to confuse the effects of race and class, and any attempt to specify the significance of race in the socialization process and outcome will need to be cautious about such confusion. Since the general patterns described earlier are found among the total population, the safest approach is to assume that similar class-related patterns would be found among blacks and to look for *further* differences associated with race. To do this, one needs to look at black-white differences *within* social class levels rather than make simple black-white population comparisons. Unfortunately, this kind of analysis, controlling for social class, has not been carried out very often. There is sufficient evidence available, however, to suggest that *much* of the overall black-white difference is in fact a social class difference; but it is equally clear that there are racial differences as well.

Family Structure

The most frequently cited difference between blacks and whites in the

---

[1] Some of the reports to be referred to actually compare blacks and nonblacks (that is, whites and others who are not Negro) while others compare whites and nonwhites. When reference is made to blacks, therefore, the specific reference is sometimes Negroes and sometimes all nonwhites. The predominance of Negroes in the nonwhite category, however, makes the outcome basically the same in both cases.

United States that is relevant to socialization is the difference in the positions of the mother and father in the family. Many authors refer to the "matriarchy" or the "matricentric structure" of the black family. There is, indeed, firm basis for emphasizing racial differences in this area. Less than one-tenth of white families are headed by a female, compared with almost three-tenths of black families. The contrast is even greater when families with children under 6 years of age are considered, the percentages being 6 percent for whites and 28 percent for blacks. Of white children under 18 years of age, 89 percent live with both parents and 8 percent live with only their mother; among blacks, the comparable figures are 59 percent and 29 percent respectively. Such differences are particularly striking in the lower classes. Of course, more blacks than whites (31 percent versus 10 percent) live below the poverty level. At that low level, 36 percent of the white and 56 percent of the black children live in families with a female head. There is a general tendency, among both blacks and whites, for the poorest families to be headed by women, but this is more prevalent among blacks. (U.S. Census, P-20, Nos. 168, 200, 204; U.S. Labor, No. 120.)

Black married women at all income levels are more likely to be working even when their husbands are present. The differences are especially striking among women with small children. Among white women with children under 6 and husbands who earn less than $3,000, 30 percent work; the comparable figure for black women is 46 percent. Even where the husband has a good income, a difference is found. Among white women with small children and husbands who earn $10,000 or more, 18 percent work; the comparable figure for black women is 26 percent. (U.S. Labor, No. 120.)

Whether one may justifiably move from such statistics to the statement that black families are matriarchal or matricentric is a more controversial question. There is no controversy with regard to the father-absent families, of course, but it is usually claimed that even when the father is present, the mother tends to be the dominant parent in black families. Such a situation is usually explained by the more secure position the black woman has had in American society throughout this century (Frazier, 1966). Her position in the labor force has tended to be more stable than her husband's, and thus she has been able to provide more dependable support for the family. The marginal position of the black man in the labor force has led not only to high rates of unemployment but also to a pervasive sense of hopelessness with respect to his ability to perform the male breadwinner role (Liebow, 1967; Parker and Kleiner, 1969). Blood and Wolfe (1969) report that female dominance is more common among black than among white working-class families in Detroit, and black wives show more autonomy and self-reliance than whites. Conversely, black husbands are less companionable to their wives than are white husbands, and the wives evaluate them less favorably as marriage partners than do white wives. Aldous

(1969) also finds that the lower-class black father is especially likely to withdraw from effective participation in the family if his wife works. Thus, the high proportion of fatherless families and the high proportion of intact families in which the mother works, in combination with such findings about the quality of family relations among blacks, suggest that the family patterns experienced by many black children are different in significant respects from those experienced by most white children.

Although such differences are probably more common at the lower social levels, they are rather well documented. There are those who are still skeptical, however, such as Hyman and Reed (1969), who find no real differences between blacks and whites in some major surveys. Others point out that segregation of husband-wife roles and minimal involvement of the father in the family are common characteristics of lower-class families, white or black. Such skepticism is worthy of consideration and suggests that further careful analysis is needed. Our present state of knowledge, however, seems to justify the tentative conclusion that the fact of being black does have an effect on family structure *in addition to* the fact of being lower class, although the extent of that effect is difficult to specify.

Family Socialization

There are evidently many similarities between black and white child-rearing patterns within a given social class (Kamii and Radin, 1967), but the black parent has to deal with one issue not faced by white parents—the fact of blackness itself. The black child learns well before going to school that he is black and that his color "makes a difference." The evidence is quite clear with respect to the general reaction to racial identity. There is a strong tendency for the black child to adopt the view of blackness that is dominant in the larger society. It is apparent that most black children do not like being black, and evidence of low self-esteem and even a hostile rejection of self is widely reported. Because such a view of blackness and of oneself as a black person is developed very early, it is not learned from the society at large. It is clearly the result of his experience in his family and in his immediate (usually wholly black) neighborhood. Why should this be so? The black parent is, of course, faced with a dilemma. While on the one hand he would want his child to develop a strong positive view of himself, he must prepare the child to cope with the fact of racial distinctions in the larger society. His direct teaching may thus be of a mixed nature. At the same time, his own marginal position in the society and his reaction to this position colors his own behavior and provides a weak model for his child. Even though the research in this area has not fully dealt with the problem of social class differences, there seems little doubt that being black contributes strongly to a negative self-image (Proshansky and Newton, 1968).

Other personality differences between black and white children seem to be associated with this dominant fact of the black self-image. In black children, the sense of inadequacy, together with the awareness of being disadvantaged, seem to lead to a withdrawn and often fearful reaction to other people. Some have pointed out that the black person's position in society generates anger in him but also requires that he repress such feelings, and this repression lowers his "potential for affectivity" (Kardiner and Ovesey, 1962). This is consistent with the finding that black children are often more passive, withdrawn, and fearful than white children and that when they are aggressive it is likely to be in a covert manner (Deutsch, 1960). This repression and poor self-image are undoubtedly also related to the finding (Rosen, 1959) that black children exhibit lower levels of need for achievement than white children.

These effects of being black seem to be especially pronounced among boys. The inadequacy of male role models in the black family, especially at lower social levels, makes socialization into the adult male role particularly difficult. Much of the black youth's exaggerated toughness and emphasis on all-male peer groups may be better understood in light of the position of the black lower-class male in our society. Even the delinquent activities of such peer groups may be seen as a means of striking back at a society that places them in such an untenable position (Drake, 1965). Although full participation in such activities does not normally begin for the boy until after he has been in school for some time, older brothers, neighborhood gangs, and an ineffectual or absent father are part of his social experience from the beginning. In contrast, the girl is likely to have as a model a mother (and often a grandmother) who is the stable center of family life. Comparatively speaking, therefore, the black girl is in a more favorable situation.

Elementary School

As is the case with all children, the black child is likely to begin school with fellow students who are of his same social class. (He is also likely to go to a predominantly or completely black school.) In many respects, therefore, he faces much the same situation as any lower-class child. One of the difficulties faced by the lower-class child, discussed in Chapter 4, is the fact that the language he has learned to speak is somewhat different from that of the dominant middle-class segment of society. The lower-class black child is even more likely than his white counterpart to speak a form of English that is different from that of his teacher. A number of studies have been conducted of urban black speech patterns, and they have demonstrated distinct differences between black and white speech. Whether black speech is any more "restricted" than white lower-class speech is not clear, but the fact that black speech is different poses special problems in the school situation (Baratz and Shuy, 1969). Such race-linked language differences present an added difficulty for the teacher who speaks (and wants her students to speak) standard middle-class "elaborated" American English. How the teacher handles that problem will strongly influence the level of difficulty experienced by the child.

Given the low position of blacks in our society, the interplay between expectations and performances (discussed in Chapter 7) assumes particular importance in the black child's school experience. To the extent that teachers have low expectations for black children, relatively low performance will not be viewed as unusual or as requiring special attention. It simply confirms the expectation. The black child's sense of inferiority, his "inadequate" language, and his different background make it unlikely that he will be able to perform "up to standard" when he enters school. Such confirmation of low expectations will not only establish them as the anticipated level for him as an individual; it will also encourage such an expectation of other black children. It may also be that such expectations are self-fulfilling, in that the teacher may behave so as to make it unlikely that the black child will be able to perform to the full extent of his capacity (Rosenthal and Jacobson, 1968).

There is some evidence of differences in the degree of academic emphasis in the schools attended by black and white children. Problems of discipline seem to be much more severe in black lower-class schools than in white lower-class schools. Deutsch (1960), for instance, reported that twice as much of the class time was devoted to disciplinary and other non-academic activities in black schools than in comparable predominantly white schools in New York City. It is difficult to determine whether this is because of the strangeness of the school situation for black students, their greater responsiveness to peer influences, or the teacher's overreaction to her expectation of trouble. Whatever its cause, such a difference is likely to have a considerable influence on how much and how well the children learn in school.

Such a combination of circumstances does not bode well for the academic progress of the black child, and there is evidence of increasing differences in the level of academic performance of black and white children as they move through the early school years. For instance, Coleman, Campbell, et al (1966) found that on the average, black children were about one and one-half years behind white children on a series of achievement tests by the time they reached the sixth grade. Black students also more often fall behind in grade level. For instance, eight-year-old children are normally in the third grade, but 24 percent of black boys and 20 percent of white boys are at least a year behind. By the time they are 11 years old (when they should be in the sixth grade), 41 percent of black boys and 26 percent of white boys are at least a year behind. The comparable figures for girls are 19 percent and 15 percent at age 8 and 29 percent and 17 percent at age 11 (U.S. Census, P-20, No. 206). Thus, although black children are behind at the beginning, they tend to become progressively farther behind as they get older. This seems especially true for black boys.

It is difficult to evaluate such findings in light of the massive social class differences between blacks and whites. One may well argue that the differences are actually class rather than race differences, or at least one may argue that the differences by race would not be nearly so great if class were taken into account. This view is supported by at least one limited study, which shows increasing class differences as students move from first to fifth grades but very small differences between the races within social class levels (Whiteman and Deutsch, 1968). It is also true that the overall race differences seem to be most pronounced in the South and Southwest and in rural areas and are much less apparent in northern, western and urban parts of the country (Coleman, Campbell, et al., 1966). Thus, although it seems probable that race, as such, makes a difference in academic achievement among young children, the evidence is not wholly adequate.

Secondary School

Similar progressive deficits in academic achievement are found among blacks as they move through secondary school. By the ninth grade, blacks are approximately two and one-fourth years behind whites on a series of achievement tests, and by the twelfth grade, the difference is about three and one-fourth years (Coleman, Campbell, et al., 1966). By 15 years of age, 44 percent of black boys and 34 percent of black girls are at least a grade behind, compared with 26 percent of white boys and 18 percent of white girls (U.S. Census, P-20, No. 206). Such findings are, of course, subject to the same questions as those for elementary school children. How much of the difference is due to class and regional differences and how much to race as such is difficult to determine.

The analysis by Coleman, Campbell, et al. (1966) does shed some light on race differences in the achievement *process,* however. They report the association between a number of variables and the achievement test performance of whites and blacks. They find that at sixth, ninth, and twelfth grade levels, the social class of origin is more closely related to test performance for whites than it is for blacks, and the difference increases as the youngsters move through the grades. That is, class of origin makes a greater difference in the performance of white children than of black children. In addition, there is a striking difference between blacks and whites in other factors associated with academic performance, holding class of origin constant. The youngster's self-concept (how competent he thinks he is) is much more clearly associated with performance for whites than for blacks. In contrast, the youngster's view of his ability to control his environment is much more clearly associated with performance for blacks than for whites. This difference is found in both the North and the South. Thus, the view of his environment, how "open" and manipulable it seems to be, is more important to the black child than is his view of his own competence.

Another finding of this same study fits well into the earlier discussion of the role of the family in the socialization of the black child. There is a much clearer association between the characteristics of the school setting (the quality of teachers and fellow students especially) and achievement among blacks than among whites. The impact of influences outside the family thus seems to be much greater for black children than for white children. A similar finding is reported by Gerson (1966), who shows that black adolescents, especially black boys, are more responsive to television as a source of socialization influences than are whites.

One other type of finding is relevant here, although the evidence is not wholly consistent. A number of studies (reviewed by Proshansky and Newton, 1968) seem to show that the aspiration levels (especially for education) of black adolescents are as high as or higher than those of whites. On the other hand, these studies also seem to show that those aspirations are "unrealistic" in that the black youngsters less often take the necessary steps toward reaching the goals they say they have set. It is not uncommon to find black high school students who say they want (or plan) to go to college but who are not enrolled in the college preparatory program, nor is it uncommon to find those who say they do not want (or plan) to go to college but who say they expect to enter an occupation that requires a college education. Undoubtedly some of the responses simply reflect wishful thinking, but it is also likely that black children on the average are less aware of what steps are necessary to accomplish their goals.

Reaching Adulthood

Not surprisingly, a higher proportion of blacks than whites drop out of high school before graduating. Nam, Rhodes, and Herriott (1968) found, for instance, that 16 percent of 16- and 17-year-old black boys were not in school and had not graduated from high school, compared with 10 percent of white boys. The comparable figures for girls were 17 percent and 9 percent for blacks and whites, respectively. However, when they controlled for social class, place of residence (South-North and rural-urban), and religion, the differences by race were reduced to less than 2 percent for both sexes. In contrast, differences between white-collar and blue-collar youngsters were about 10 percent for both sexes, even after controlling on the other variables, including race. In other words, the differences by social class seem to be much more significant than the differences by race, although race does make a difference over and above the other variables.

As suggested in the previous section, those blacks who are in school at age 15 are more likely than whites to be at a lower grade level than they should be at their age. The same is true at older ages. Blacks are less likely than whites to be in school in the 18 to 21 age period (56 percent of white men, 40 percent of black men, 34 percent of white women, 30 percent of black women are in school). In addition, however, to those who are in school in that age range, whites are more likely to be in college (85 percent of white men, 57 percent of black men, 89 percent of white women, 70 percent of black women who are in school are in college). Blacks are less likely than whites to graduate from high school (56 percent versus 77 percent), and of those who do graduate, blacks are less likely to go to college (33 percent versus 45 percent). (U.S. Census, P-20, Nos. 194 and 206). These differences are in part a function of the fact that, in general, youngsters from lower-class origins get less education than those from higher-class origins. However, Spady (1967) has shown that at all levels of origin whites attain higher levels of education than blacks.

The same pattern is found when occupational attainment is studied. Blau and Duncan (1967) found that, even though blacks generally begin life at lower social class levels than whites, they are more likely than whites to be downwardly mobile and less likely to be upwardly mobile. Except for college-educated blacks, in fact, the greater the amount of education black men receive the greater the difference between their occupational level and that of white men with similar amounts of education. This seems to mean that all men are limited to lower occupations if they do not have much education, but black men do not obtain the same occupational advantage whites do from additional education. Siegel (1965) has shown that the same is true for income—the higher the level of education, the greater the income differential between blacks and whites. Thus, blacks tend to enter the labor force earlier than whites, they enter at a lower level, their lower social class of origin does not prevent them from being downwardly mobile, and their educational achievement does not insure their being upwardly mobile.

Becoming an adult also involves becoming a spouse and a parent. Blacks enter adulthood earlier by this definition also. There is a tendency for black women to engage in premarital sexual relations more than white women, but the difference is found primarily within the lower class. Out-of-wedlock conceptions are more common among blacks, and when an illegitimate birth occurs, the black mother is more likely than the white to keep her child. White women are more likely to obtain an abortion in the case of an out-of-wedlock conception (Gebhard, Pomeroy, Martin, and Christenson, 1958). As a result of this, even among women who do get married, it is much more common for black women to be pregnant and possibly have a child before marriage. Over one-fourth of black wives have a child before marriage, compared with only 4 percent of whites. Although wives with less education are more likely to have a child before marriage, at all educational levels black wives are much more likely to do so. Age at first marriage does not differ strikingly by race, but there is a much greater tendency for black couples to break up during the first few years of marriage. (U.S. Census, P-20, No. 186.) This pattern again points up the centrality of the black woman. Her early maternal responsibilities, together with the instability of her marriage, put her in a position of having greater responsibility for her children than is usual for the white woman.

It is not possible to trace these family patterns back to the social class of the young couple's parents, so one cannot be certain that the greater illegitimacy and marital instability are associated with race as such rather than social class of origin. They are associated with the achieved social level of the young couple, greater instability being found at the lower levels, but the weak relationship between origin and achieved status among blacks leaves us in doubt about how much of the instability can be explained by lower-class origins rather than racial identity. The black-white differences are so massive, however, that it seems highly improbable that the lower-class origins of blacks can explain them entirely.

The picture that emerges, therefore, is one of lower educational attainment, lower occupational attainment, and greater instability of family life for the young black adult. Although differences are found between blacks and whites in the early stages of their development, these differences in early adulthood seem to be more massive. Most striking of all is the fact that, even when blacks *do* achieve a relatively high position within the educational and occupational systems, the rewards they obtain from that achievement are lower than those obtained by whites. In the next section, this single fact will be used as a basis for integrating the observations that have been made up to this point.

Overview

One of the basic themes in the body of this book is that educational attainment is the primary means of social mobility in this society. The major avenue of access to higher occupational positions and the greater income they provide is through increased levels of education. The position taken in Chapter 7 is that educational attainment depends on adequate performance in the early stages of the educational process and that the incremental nature of education makes later opportunities increasingly dependent on earlier performance. At the same time, it is suggested there that social class influences the process of achievement in two ways—through providing a set of significant others who influence the kinds of characteristics the individual develops, and through establishing a set of expectations these others communicate to the individual. Although the expectations others have must come to terms with the actual performance of the individual, it is equally true that the individual's behavior must take the expectations into account. The expectations become particularly constraining if they are not subject to alteration in light of the individual's performance. If the opportunity structure is indeed an "open" one, early performance not only should determine later expectations, but should influence the number and kinds of opportunities open to the individual in the future. It has been suggested that expectations and opportunities may be less than fully responsive to the performance of lower-class children, but it seems certain that they are not fully responsive to the performance of black children.

Perhaps the best way to summarize the basis for such a statement is to present the results of an analysis carried out by Duncan (1969). That analysis pursues systematically the argument that says: Socialization processes and outcomes are the same for blacks and whites, but the fact that the black population has a different *distribution* of the significant *background* characteristics than the white population leads to a different *distribution* of *outcomes*. The Duncan analysis says, in effect, that we can estimate what the black-white differences in outcome *would be* if the distribution of background characteristics of the two races were the same. For instance, lower-class families tend to be larger than higher-class families, and black families tend to be lower class. Since children who are in the lower class and are in larger families generally have lower educational attainment, perhaps the black-white differences in educational attainment can be explained by these differences in class and family size. Similarly, since individuals from lower-class origins, from larger families, and with lower educational attainment get poorer jobs, perhaps we can explain black-white differences in occupational placement by these three background variables. Finally, since people from lower-class origins, from larger families, with low educational attainment and poor jobs get less pay, perhaps we can explain black-white income differences as due to these four background variables. Such an approach makes it possible to estimate the cumulative effect of this series of background factors for outcomes in education, occupation, and income.

TABLE A.1

EXPLANATION OF BLACK-WHITE DIFFERENCES IN EDUCATION, OCCUPATION, AND INCOME, USING BACKGROUND VARIABLES*

	Outcomes		
Explanatory Variables	Years of School Completed	Occupation Score	Income in Dollars
	(W) 11.7	(W) 43.5	(W) 7,070
Social level of origin	1.0	6.6	940
Number of siblings	0.1	0.6	70
Years of school completed	1.2	4.8	520
	(B) 9.4		
Occupation prestige score		11.8	830
		(B) 19.7	
Income in dollars			1,430
			(B) 3,280
Total black-white difference	2.3	23.8	3,790

* Adapted from "Inheritance of Poverty or Inheritance of Race?" by Otis Dudley Duncan. Table 6 of *On Understanding Poverty*, edited by Daniel P. Moynihan, Basic Books, Inc., Publishers, New York, 1969. Based on data collected from a national sample of native-born men with nonfarm backgrounds, 25 to 64 years of age, in March 1962. (B) and (W) stand for black and white, respectively.

Table A.1 reports the results of the analysis for a 1962 national sample of men from nonfarm origins. A careful look at the last column (Income) will help the reader understand the analysis. In that column it is reported that the average income for whites the previous year (1961) was $7,070, and for blacks it was $3,280. The difference between the means (reported in the "Total" row) is $3,790. Moving down the last column, the numbers represent the amount of the difference between black and white income levels that can be attributed to a particular background difference between the two races. For instance, if the distributions of social origins of blacks and whites were somehow made the same and everything else remained as it is, it is estimated that the income difference would be reduced by $940. Similarly, if, *in addition,* the size of black and white families were actually the same instead of black families being larger, the income difference would be reduced by another $70. Equating blacks and whites on *all four* of these background variables (social origin, family size, educational attainment, and level of occupation), the income difference between the races would be reduced by $2,360. Thus, it does follow that much of the black-white difference in income can be attributed to these background differences.

Similarly, moving to the columns to the left, the difference in the average prestige scores of the occupations held by blacks and whites (a total of 23.8 points as reported in the "Total" row), can be partially explained by the three prior variables (social origin, family size, and educational attainment). Of the total difference of 23.8 points, 6.6 points can be explained by differences in social origin. If family size and educational attainment are considered in addition to origin, another 5.4 points (0.6 plus 4.8) can be explained. Finally, differences in educational attainment can be partially explained by social origin and family size.

The important point for our purposes, however, is that *at each point in the analysis large residual differences remain.* These are represented by the last number in each column to the right of the brackets. More than one-third of the income differential ($1,430), more than one-half of the occupational prestige differential (11.8 points), and more than one-half of the educational attainment differential (1.2 years of schooling) are *not* explained by the variables used in the analysis. For us, therefore, the most significant thing is that social origin does not, even in combination with the individual's own achievement, explain the differences in outcome. Even when blacks are "successful" by the core criteria of success in this society, they do not receive the same rewards for that achievement as whites receive.

It may be argued that this very significant outcome has an important feedback effect on the whole process we have been examining. In fact, the findings reviewed in this appendix suggest that this is so. Black men, who receive fewer rewards than whites for their achievements, are less likely to provide a stable paternal influence within the family. Young black children, especially boys, find black identity unattractive and suffer from the pressure of an unacceptable self-image. Among other things, they exhibit lower levels of need for achievement than whites. Black children, especially boys, rapidly fall behind in school. These same black children's academic achievement reflects more clearly than does that of white children their view of the environment as threatening and intractable. They are more likely than whites to agree with the statements provided them by Coleman, Campbell, et al (1968): "Good luck is more important than hard work for success"; "Every time I try to get ahead, something or somebody stops me"; "People like me don't have much of a chance to be successful in life." These are the children of the men Blau and Duncan (1967) show are more likely to be downwardly mobile in spite of the fact that they started out lower than whites to begin with. These are the children of the men (and women) who receive poorer jobs at any level of educational attainment and lower pay for whatever job they have. These children may even be aware that this is *especially* true if they have been "successful" in their educational and occupational achievement efforts.

One does not have to turn to a psychiatric analysis of such children to explain their behavior. This is hardly a case of paranoia. There is a very real empirical basis for believing that achievement striving does not pay, that the system does not respond to everyone according to the same standards. One can hardly be surprised that black children (and their parents) have high aspirations but very little idea about how to achieve these lofty goals.

There seems only one remaining way to bring these observations somewhat more into line with a belief in racial equality of opportunity. That is an appeal to innate differences in ability between the races. Such a claim is given substance by the fact that the general performance of blacks on tests we call "intelligence tests" is lower than that of whites. It is hardly debatable, however, that performance on such tests depends on both innate and learned factors, and it is extremely difficult to tease these two components apart. The great majority of experts in the field, however, tend to agree with Gottesman (1968, p. 46) when he concludes his discussion of this issue by saying: "At the present time Negro and white differences in general intelligence in the United States appear to be primarily associated with differences in environmental advantages." The restraint with which such experts state their conclusions makes it possible for those who would grasp at the straw of innate black inferiority to continue to do so.

A number of results of research reviewed in this volume make the straw less worthy of the grasp, however. For instance, it has been shown that the academic performance of blacks is generally much more responsive than that of whites to variations in their social surroundings (for example, the quality of their peers and teachers). It seems odd that those who might be thought of as less intelligent would be *more* responsive, since such responsiveness is the usual definition of intelligence. Also, the adult social position of a black man is *less* predictable from his social origins than is the position of a white man. One might have expected that, if innate differences were of prime importance, the outcome should be very predictable for *both* races. Finally, even ignoring all this, how does one fit into a genetic explanation the fact that even when blacks *do* achieve according to the standards of the society, they are not rewarded in the same way as whites? It is hard to avoid concluding that something else is involved.

Although the "opportunity structure" has been alluded to within the body of this report, it has assumed less centrality than seems to be warranted in the present discussion. It has been noted earlier, however, that the upward mobility in this country over the past few generations seems to be at least as much a function of the changes in the occupational structure as it is a function of the successful striving of individuals. The data in Table A.1 suggest that whatever the case may be for the majority of Americans, black Americans are less likely to be "pulled up" by such structural changes. In fact, they are not very likely to move up in the status hierarchy even when they have done all the "right" things—like get a good education. Clearly there are sizeable differences in the paths blacks and whites follow to maturity. It may be that many of these differences can be explained by means of differences in the socialization experiences of blacks and whites. Beyond such a socialization explanation, however, lies that "something else" that gives empirical substance to the statement blacks find so much more acceptable than whites: "People like me don't have much of a chance to be successful in life."

BIBLIOGRAPHY

ADAMS, B. N. and MEIDAM, M. T. 1968. Economics, family structure, and college attendance. *American Journal of Sociology. 74*: 230–39.

ALDOUS, J. 1969. Wives' employment status and lower-class men as husband-fathers: Support for the Moynihan thesis. *Journal of Marriage and the Family. 31*: 469–76.

ALEXANDER, C. N. and CAMPBELL, E. Q. 1964. Peer influences on adolescent educational aspirations and attainments. *American Sociological Review. 29*: 568–75.

ALMOND, G. and VERBA, S. 1963. *The civic culture: Political attitudes and democracy in five nations.* Princeton, N.J.: Princeton University Press.

ARONFREED, J. 1969. The concept of internalization. In *Handbook of socialization theory and research*, ed. D. A. Goslin. Chicago: Rand McNally & Co.

BANDURA, A. and WALTERS, R. H. 1963. *Social learning and personality development.* New York: Holt, Rinehart & Winston, Inc.

BARATZ, J. and SHUY, R. 1969. *Teaching black children to read.* Washington, D.C.: Center for Applied Linguistics.

BARCLAY, A. and CUSUMANO, D. R. 1967. Father absence, cross-sex identity, and field dependent behavior in male adolescents. *Child Development. 38*: 243–50.

BAYER, A. E. 1969. Life plans and marriage age: An application of path analysis. *Journal of Marriage and the Family. 31*: 551–58.

BECKER, H. S. 1952. Social class variations in the teacher-pupil relationship. *Journal of Educational Sociology. 25*: 451–65.

BECKER, W. C. 1964. Consequences of different kinds of parental discipline. In *Review of child development research* Vol. 1, ed. M. H. Hoffman and L. W. Hoffman. New York: Russell Sage Foundation.

BEREITER, C. and ENGELMANN, S. 1966. *Teaching disadvantaged children in the preschool.* Englewood Cliffs, N.J.: Prentice-Hall, Inc.

BERNARD, J. 1964. The adjustments of married mates. In *Handbook of marriage and the family*, ed. H. T. Christensen. Chicago: Rand McNally & Co.

BERNSTEIN, B. 1964. Elaborated and restricted codes: Their social origins and some consequences. In *The Ethnography of Communication*, ed. J. J. Gumpery and D. Hymes. Special publication of the *American Anthropologist. 66*: 55–69. Nov. 6, pt. 2.

BIDWELL, C. A. 1965. The school as a formal organization. In *Handbook of Organizations*, ed. J. E. March. Chicago: Rand McNally & Co.

BLAU, P. M. and DUNCAN, O. D. 1967. *The American occupational structure.* New York: John Wiley & Sons, Inc.

BLOOD, R. O., JR. and WOLFE, D. M. 1969. Negro-white differences in blue-collar marriages in a northern metropolis. *Social Forces. 48*: 59–64.

BOWERMAN, C. E. and KINCH, J. W. 1959. Changes in family and peer orientation of children between the fourth and tenth grades. *Social Forces. 37*: 206–11.

BOWERS, P. and LONDON, P. 1965. Developmental correlates of role-playing ability. *Child Development. 36*: 499–508.

BRIM, O. G., JR. 1959. *Education for child rearing.* New York: Russell Sage Foundation.

———. 1966. Socialization through the life cycle. In *Socialization after childhood*, O. G. Brim, Jr. and S. Wheeler. New York: John Wiley & Sons, Inc.

BRITTAIN, C. V. 1963. Adolescent choices and parent-peer cross pressures. *American Sociological Review. 28*: 385–90.

BRODY, G. F. 1968. Socioeconomic differences in stated maternal child-rearing practices and in observed maternal behavior. *Journal of Marriage and the Family. 30*: 656–60.

BRONFENBRENNER, U. 1958. Socialization and social class through time and space. In *Readings in social psychology*, ed. E. E. Maccoby, T. M. Newcomb, and E. L. Hartley. New York: Holt, Rinehart & Winston, Inc. Pp. 400–25.

———. 1970. *Two worlds of childhood.* New York: Russell Sage Foundation. Chap. 5.

BROWN, D. G. 1957. Masculinity-femininity development in children. *Journal of consulting psychology. 21*: 197–202.

BROWN, R. W., 1958. *Words and things.* New York: The Free Press.

BURCHINAL, L. G. 1964. The premarital dyad and love involvement. In *Hand-*

book of marriage and the family, ed. H. T. Christensen. Chicago: Rand McNally & Co.

CAMPBELL, E. Q. 1969. Adolescent socialization. In *Handbook of socialization theory and research*, ed. D. A. Goslin. Chicago: Rand McNally & Co.

CAMPBELL, J. D. 1964. Peer relations in childhood. In *Review of child development research*, ed. M. L. Hoffman and L. Hoffman. New York: Russell Sage Foundation.

CARLSON, R. O. 1961. Variation and myth in social status of teachers. *Journal of Educational Sociology. 35*: 104–18.

————. 1964. Environmental constraints and organizational consequences: The public school and its clients. In *Behavioral Science and Educational Administration Yearbook*, ed. D. E. Griffiths. National Society of the Study of Education.

CHOMSKY, N. 1967. The formal nature of language. In *Biological foundations of language*, E. H. Lenneberg. New York: John Wiley & Sons, Inc.

CICOUREL, A. V. and KITSUSE, J. I. 1963. *The educational decision-makers*. Indianapolis: The Bobbs-Merrill Co., Inc.

CLAUSEN, J. A. 1966. Family structure, socialization, and personality. In *Review of child development research*, Vol. II, ed. L. Hoffman and M. Hoffman. New York: Russell Sage Foundation.

————. 1968. *Socialization and society*. Boston: Little, Brown & Company.

COLEMAN, J. S. 1961. *The adolescent society*. New York: The Free Press.

COLEMAN, J. S., CAMPBELL, E. Q. et al. 1966. *Equality of educational opportunity*. Washington, D. C.: Government Printing Office.

COOLEY, C. H. 1902. *Human nature and the social order*. New York: Charles Scribner's Sons.

COOPERSMITH, S. 1967. *The antecedents of self-esteem*. San Francisco: W. H. Freeman and Co., Publishers.

COSTANZO, P. R. and SHAW, M. E. 1970. Conformity as a function of age level. In *Perspectives in child psychology*, ed. T. Spencer and N. Kass. New York: McGraw-Hill Book Company.

COTTRELL, L. S., JR. 1969. Interpersonal interaction and the development of the self. In *Handbook of socialization theory and research*, ed. D. A. Goslin. Chicago: Rand McNally & Co.

COWAN, P. A. 1967. The link between cognitive structure and social structure. Paper presented to Society for Research in Child Development, March 1967.

DAVIDSON, H. H. and LANG, G. 1960. Children's perceptions of their teachers' feelings toward them related to self-perception, school achievement and behavior. *Journal of Experimental Education. 29*: 107–18.

DAVIS, J. A. 1965. *Undergraduate career decisions*. Chicago: Aldine Publishing Company.

DENTLER, R. A. and WARSHAUSER, M. E. 1965. *Big city dropouts and illiterates*. New York: Center for Urban Education.

DEUTSCH, M., 1960. *Minority group and class status as related to social and personality factors in scholastic achievement*, Monograph No. 2. Ithaca, New York: Society of Applied Anthropology.

DOUVAN, E. and ADELSON, J. 1958. The psychodynamics of social mobility in adolescent boys. *Journal of Abnormal and Social Psychology. 56*: 31–44.

———. 1966. *The adolescent experience.* New York: John Wiley & Sons, Inc.

DRAKE, ST. C. 1965. The social and economic status of the negro in the United States. *Daedalus. 94*: 771–814.

DUNCAN, O. D. 1961. A socioeconomic index for all occupations. In A. J. Reiss, Jr., et al., *Occupations and Social Status.* New York: The Free Press.

———. 1968. Ability and achievement. *Eugenics Quarterly. 15*: 1–11.

———. 1969. Inheritance of poverty or inheritance of race? In *On understanding poverty: Perspectives from the social sciences,* ed. D. P. Moynihan. New York: Basic Books, Inc., Publishers.

DUNCAN, O. D., HALLER, A. O. and PORTES, A. 1968. Peer influences on aspirations: A reinterpretation. *American Journal of Sociology. 74*: 119–37.

DUVALL, E. M. 1946. Conceptions of parenthood. *American Journal of Sociology. 52*: 193–203.

ECKLAND, B. K. 1964. Social class and college graduation: Some misconceptions corrected. *American Journal of Sociology. 70*: 36–50.

EISENSTADT, S. N. 1956. *From generation to generation.* New York: The Free Press.

ELDER, G. H. 1962. Structural variations in the child-rearing relationship. *Sociometry. 25*: 241–62.

———. 1963. Parental power legitimation and its effect on the adolescent. *Sociometry. 26*: 50–65.

———. 1969. Appearance and education in marriage mobility. *American Sociological Review. 34*: 519–33.

ENTWISLE, D. R. 1968. Developmental sociolinguistics: Inner-city children. *American Journal of Sociology. 74*: 37–49.

FAGOT, B. I. and PATTERSON, G. R. 1969. An in vivo analysis of reinforcing contingencies for sex-role behaviors in the pre-school child. *Developmental Psychology. 1*: 563–68.

FEFFER, M. H. and GOUREVITCH, V. 1960. Cognitive aspects of role-taking in children. *Journal of Personality. 28*: 383–96.

FINDLAY, D. C. and MCGUIRE, C. 1957. Social status and abstract behavior. *Journal of Abnormal and Social Psychology. 54*: 135–47.

FOLGER, J. K. and NAM, C. B. 1967. *Education of the American population.* Washington, D.C.: Government Printing Office.

FRAZIER, E. F. 1966. *The Negro family in the United States.* Chicago: University of Chicago Press.

GEBHARD, P. H., POMEROY, W., MARTIN, C. and CHRISTENSON, C. 1958. *Pregnancy, birth and abortion.* New York: Harper & Row, Publishers.

GERSON, W. M. 1966. Mass media socialization behavior: Negro-white differences. *Social Forces. 45*: 40–50.

GERTH, H. H. and MILLS, C. W. 1946. *From Max Weber: Essays in sociology.* New York: Oxford University Press.

GILDEA, M., GLIDEWELL, J. and KANTOR, M. 1961. Maternal attitudes and the general adjustment in school children. In *Parental Attitudes and Child Behavior,* ed. J. Glidewell. Springfield, Ill.: Charles C. Thomas, Publisher.

GOLDSTEIN, B. 1967. *Low income youth in urban areas.* New York: Holt, Rinehart & Winston, Inc.

GOSLIN, D. A. 1965. *The school in contemporary society.* Chicago: Scott, Foresman & Company.

————, ed. 1969. *Handbook of socialization theory and research.* Chicago: Rand McNally & Co.

GOTTESMAN, I. I. 1968. Biogenetics of race and class. In *Social Class, Race, and Psychological Development.* ed. M. Deutsch, I. Katz, and A. R. Jensen. New York: Holt, Rinehart & Winston, Inc.

GREEN, A. W. 1946. The middle class male child and neurosis. *American Sociological Review. 11*: 31–41.

GREENFIELD, P. M. and BRUNER, J. S. 1969. Culture and cognitive growth. In *Handbook of Socialization Theory and Research*, ed. D. A. Goslin. Chicago: Rand McNally & Co.

GURIN, G., VEROFF, J. and FELD, S. 1960. *Americans view their mental health: A nationwide interview survey.* New York: Basic Books, Inc., Publishers.

HAN, W. S. 1968. Discrepancy in socioeconomic level of aspiration and perception of illegitimate expediency. *American Journal of Sociology. 74*: 240–47.

HARTUP, W. and CHARLESWORTH, R. 1967. Positive social reinforcement in the nursery peer group. *Child Development. 38*: 993–1002.

HENRY, J. 1955. Docility, or giving teach what she wants. *Journal of Social Issues. 2*: 33–41.

HESS, R. and SHIPMAN, V. 1965. Early experience and the socialization of cognitive modes in children. *Child Development. 36*: 869–86.

HICKERSON, N. 1966. *Education for alienation.* Englewood Cliffs, N.J.: Prentice-Hall, Inc.

HODGE, R. W., SIEGEL, P. M. and ROSSI, P. H. 1964. Occupational prestige in the United States, 1925–63, *American Journal of Sociology. 70*: 286–302.

HOFFMAN, M. L. 1969. Moral development. In *Manual of Child Psychology*, ed. P. Mussen. New York: John Wiley & Sons, Inc.

HOFFMAN, M. L. and SALTZSTEIN, H. D. 1967. Parent discipline and the child's moral development. *Journal of Personality and Social Psychology. 5*: 45–57.

HOLLINGSHEAD, A. B. 1950. Cultural factors in the selection of marriage mates. *American Sociological Review. 15*: 619–27.

HOLLINGSHEAD, A. B. and REDLICH, F. C. 1958. *Social class and mental illness: A community study.* New York: John Wiley & Sons, Inc.

HUGHES, M. C. 1953. Sex differences in reading achievement in the elementary grades. *Supplementary Educational Monographs*, No. 77. Pp. 102–106.

HYMAN, H. H. 1953. The value systems of different classes: A social psychological contribution to the analysis of stratification. In *Class, Status & Power*, ed. R. Bendix and S. M. Lipset. New York: The Free Press.

HYMAN, H. H. and REED, J. S. 1969. "Black matriarchy" reconsidered: Evidence from secondary analysis of sample surveys. *Public Opinion Quarterly. 33*: 346–54.

IRELAN, L. M. 1966. *Low-income life styles.* Washington, D.C.: Government Printing Office.

JACKSON, B. and MARSDEN, D. 1962. *Education and the working class.* London: Routledge & Kegan Paul Ltd.

JENSEN, A. R. 1968. Social class and verbal learning. In *Social class, race and psychological development,* ed. M. Deutsch, I. Katz, and A. R. Jensen. New York: Holt, Rinehart & Winston, Inc.

JOHN, V. and GOLDSTEIN, L. S. 1964. The social context of language acquisition. *Merrill-Palmer Quarterly. 10:* 266–75.

KAGAN, J. 1964. Acquisition and significance of sex typing and sex role identity. In *Review of child development research,* Vol. I, ed. M. Hoffman and L. Hoffman. New York: Russell Sage Foundation.

KAHL, J. A. 1953. Educational and occupational aspirations of "common man" boys. *Harvard Educational Review. 23:* 186–203.

———. 1957. *The American class structure.* New York: Holt, Rinehart & Winston, Inc.

———. 1965. Some measures of achievement motivation. *American Journal of Sociology. 70:* 660–81.

KAMII, C. K. and RADIN, N. L. 1967. Class differences in the socialization practices of Negro mothers. *Journal of Marriage and the Family. 29:* 302–10.

KANDEL, D. B. and LESSER, G. S. 1969. Parental and peer influences on educational plans of adolescents. *American Sociological Review. 34:* 212–23.

KARDINER, A. and OVESEY, L. 1962. *The mark of oppression.* Cleveland: The World Publishing Company.

KERCKHOFF, A. C. 1969. Early antecedents of role-taking and role-playing ability. *Merrill-Palmer Quarterly. 15:* 229–47.

KERCKHOFF, A. C. and BEAN, F. D. 1970. Social status and interpersonal patterns among married couples. *Social Forces. 49:* 264–71.

KOHLBERG, L. 1969a. Stage and sequence: The cognitive-developmental approach to socialization. In *Handbook of Socialization Theory and Research,* ed. D. A. Goslin. Chicago: Rand McNally & Co.

———. 1969b. *Stages in the development of moral thought and action.* New York: Holt, Rinehart & Winston, Inc.

KOHN, M. L. 1959. Social class and parental values. *American Journal of Sociology. 64:* 337–51.

———. 1963. Social class and parent-child relationships: An interpretation. *American Journal of Sociology. 68:* 471–80.

———. 1969. *Class and conformity.* Homewood, Ill.: Dorsey Press.

KRAUSS, I. 1964. Sources of educational aspirations among working-class youth. *American Sociological Review. 29:* 867–79.

KRAUSS, R. M. and ROTTER, G. S. 1968. Communication abilities of children as a function of status and age. *Merrill-Palmer Quarterly. 14:* 161–73.

LAVIN, D. E. 1965. *The prediction of academic performance.* New York: Russell Sage Foundation.

LAWTON, D. 1968. *Social class, language, and education.* London: Routledge & Kegan Paul Ltd.

LEARY, T. 1957. *Interpersonal diagnosis of personality.* New York: The Ronald Press Company.

LENSKI, G. 1966. *Power and privilege: A theory of social stratification.* New York: McGraw-Hill Book Company.

LIEBOW, E. 1967. *Tally's corner.* Boston: Little, Brown & Company.

LURIA, A. R. 1966. *Higher cortical functions in man.* New York: Basic Books, Inc., Publishers.

LUSZKI, M. B. and SCHMUCK, R. 1963. Pupil perceptions of parental attitudes toward school. *Mental Hygiene. 47:* 289–99.

MACARTHUR, R. S. 1955. An experimental investigation of persistence in secondary school boys. *Canadian Journal of Psychology. 9:* 42–55.

MACCOBY, E. E. 1961. The choice of variables in the study of socialization. *Sociometry. 24:* 357–71.

————. 1968. The development of moral values and behavior in childhood. In *Socialization and Society,* ed. J. A. Clausen. Boston: Little, Brown & Company.

————, ed. 1966. *The development of sex differences.* Stanford, Calif.: Stanford University Press.

MCCARTHY, D. 1954. Language development in children. In *Manual of Child Psychology,* ed. L. Carmichael. New York: John Wiley & Sons, Inc.

MCDAVID, J. 1959. Some relationships between social reinforcement and scholastic achievement. *Journal of Consulting Psychology. 23:* 151–54.

MCDILL, E. L., RIGSBY, L. C. and MEYERS, E. D., JR. 1969. Educational climates of high schools: Their effects and sources. *American Journal of Sociology. 74:* 567–89.

MEAD, G. H. 1934. *Mind, self and society: From the standpoint of a social behaviorist.* Chicago: University of Chicago Press.

MEDINNUS, G. and JOHNSON, R. 1969. *Child and adolescent psychology.* New York: John Wiley & Sons, Inc.

MERTON, R. K. 1957. *Social theory and social research,* rev. ed. New York: The Free Press.

MILLER, S. M., SALEEM, B. L., and HERRINGTON, B. 1964. *School dropouts: A commentary and annotated bibliography.* Syracuse, N.Y.: Syracuse University Youth Development Center.

MOORE, W. E. and TUMIN, M. M. 1949. Some social functions of ignorance. *American Sociological Review. 14:* 787–95.

MYRDAL, G. (with R. Sterver and A. Rose). 1944. *An American dilemma.* New York: Harper & Row, Publishers.

NAM, C. B., RHODES, A. L., and HERRIOTT, R. E. 1968. School retention by race, religion and socioeconomic status. *Journal of Human Resources. 3:* 171–90.

NEWCOMB, T. M. 1961. *The acquaintance process.* New York: Holt, Rinehart & Winston, Inc.

PARKER, S. and KLEINER, R. J. 1969. Social and psychological dimensions of the family role performance of the Negro male. *Journal of Marriage and the Family. 31:* 500–506.

PARSONS, T. 1949. Certain primary sources and patterns of aggression in the social structure of the Western world. In *A Study of Interpersonal Relations*, ed. P. Mullahy. New York: Hermitage House.

———. 1959. The school class as a social system: Some of its functions in American society. *Harvard Educational Review. 29*: 297–318.

PIAGET, J. 1952. *The origins of intelligence in children.* New York: International Universities Press.

POPE, B. 1953. Socio-economic contrasts in children's peer culture prestige values. *Genetic Psychology Monographs. 48*: 157–220.

PROSHANSKY, H. and NEWTON, P. 1968. The nature and meaning of Negro self-identity. In *Social Class, Race, and Psychological Development*, ed. M. Deutsch, I. Katz, and A. R. Jensen. New York: Holt, Rinehart & Winston, Inc.

RAINWATER, L. 1966. Some aspects of lower class sexual behavior. *Journal of Social Issues. 22*: 96–108.

REHBERG, R. A. and SCHAFER, W. E. 1968. Participation in interscholastic athletics and college expectations. *American Journal of Sociology. 73*: 732–40.

REHBERG, R. A., SINCLAIR, J., and SCHAFER, W. E. 1970. Adolescent achievement behavior, family authority structure, and parental socialization practices. *American Journal of Sociology. 75*: 1012–34.

REISS, A. J., JR. 1965. Social organization and socialization: Variations on a theme about generations. Working paper #1, Center for Research on Social Organization, University of Michigan, Ann Arbor, Michigan. (Multilith)

REISS, A. J., JR., et al. 1961. *Occupations and social status.* New York: The Free Press.

REISS, I. L. 1960. *Premarital sexual standards in America.* New York: The Free Press.

RHEINGOLD, H. L. 1969. The social and socializing infant. In *Handbook of Socialization Theory and Research*, ed. D. A. Goslin. Chicago: Rand McNally & Co.

RODMAN, H. 1963. The lower class value stretch. *Social Forces. 42*: 205–15.

ROSEN, B. C. 1956. The achievement syndrome: A psychocultural dimension of social stratification. *American Sociological Review. 21*: 203–11.

———. 1959. Race, ethnicity, and the achievement syndrome. *American Sociological Review. 24*: 47–60.

ROSEN, B. C., CROCKETT, H. J. and NUNN, C. Z. 1969. *Achievement in American society.* Cambridge, Mass.: Schenkman Publishing Co., Inc.

ROSEN, B. C. and D'ANDRADE, R. G. 1959. The psychosocial origins of achievement motivation. *Sociometry. 22*: 185–218.

ROSENTHAL, R. and JACOBSON, L. 1968. *Pygmalion in the classroom.* New York: Holt, Rinehart & Winston, Inc.

SCHAEFER, E. S. 1959. A circumplex model of maternal behavior. *Journal of Abnormal and Social Psychology. 59*: 226–35.

SCHATZMAN, L. and STRAUSS, A. 1955. Social class and modes of communication. *American Journal of Sociology. 60*: 329–38.

SCHNEIDER, L. and LYSGAARD, S. 1953. The deferred gratification pattern: A preliminary study. *American Sociological Review. 18*: 142–49.

SCHUTZ, W. C. 1958. *FIRO: A three-dimensional theory of interpersonal behavior.* New York: Holt, Rinehart & Winston, Inc.

SCOTT, R. A. 1968. *The making of blind men.* New York: Russell Sage Foundation.

SEARS, R. R., MACCOBY, E. E., and LEVIN, H. 1957. *Patterns of child rearing.* New York: Harper & Row, Publishers.

SEBALD, H. 1968. *Adolescence: A sociological analysis.* New York: Appleton-Century-Crofts.

SECORD, P. F. and BACKMAN, C. W. 1964. *Social psychology.* New York: McGraw-Hill Book Company.

SEWELL, W. H., HALLER, A. O., and OHLENDORF, G. W. 1970. The educational and early occupational status attainment process: A replication and revision. *American Sociological Review. 35*: 1014–27.

SEWELL, W. H. and SHAH, V. P. 1967. Socioeconomic status, intelligence, and the attainment of higher education. *Sociology of Education. 40*: 1–23.

————. 1968. Social class, parental encouragement, and educational aspirations. *American Journal of Sociology. 73*: 559–72.

SEXTON, P. 1969. *The feminized male.* New York: Random House, Inc.

SHAW, M. C., EDSON, K., and BELL, H. M. 1960. The self-concept of bright underachieving high school students as revealed by an adjective check list. *Personnel and Guidance Journal. 39*: 193–96.

SHAW, M. C. and McCUEN, J. T. 1960. The onset of academic underachievement in bright children. *Journal of Educational Psychology. 51*: 103–108.

SHERIF, M., et al. 1961. *Intergroup conflict and co-operation.* Norman, Okla.: University of Oklahoma Press.

SHORT, J. F., JR., RIVERA, R., and TENNYSON, R. A. 1965. Perceived opportunities, gang membership and delinquency. *American Sociological Review. 30*: 56–67.

SIEGEL, P. M. 1965. On the cost of being a Negro. *Sociological Inquiry. 35*: 41–57.

SILLER, J. 1957. Socioeconomic status and conceptual thinking. *Journal of Abnormal and Social Psychology. 55*: 365–71.

SIMON, K. A. and GRANT, W. V. 1967. *Digest of educational statistics.* Washington, D.C.: Government Printing Office.

SMITH, M. B. 1968. Competence and socialization. In *Socialization and Society,* ed. J. A. Clausen. Boston: Little, Brown & Company.

SPADY, W. G. 1967. Educational mobility and access: Growth and paradoxes. *American Journal of Sociology. 73*: 273–86.

SPENCE, L. H. 1967. Associative clustering in culturally deprived and non-culturally deprived children. M. A. Thesis, Duke University.

SPIRO, M. E., 1958. *Children of the kibbutz.* Cambridge, Mass.: Harvard University Press.

STENDLER, C. B. 1951. Social class differences in parental attitudes toward school at grade 1 level. *Child Development. 22*: 37–46.

STENDLER, C. B. and YOUNG, N. 1950. The impact of beginning first grade upon socialization as reported by mothers. *Child Development. 21*: 241–60.

STINCHCOMBE, A. L. 1965. *Rebellion in a high school.* Chicago: Quadrangle Books.

STRAUS, M. A. 1962. Deferred gratification, social class, and the achievement syndrome. *American Sociological Review. 27*: 326–35.

STRAUSS, A. L. 1956. The learning of roles and of concepts as twin processes. *Journal of Genetic Psychology. 88*: 211–17.

STRODTBECK, F. L. 1958. Family interaction, values, and achievement. In *Talent and Society*, D. C. McClelland, et al. New York: Van Nostrand Reinhold Company.

SUGARMAN, B. 1967. Involvement in youth culture, academic achievement and conformity in school: An empirical study of London schoolboys. *The British Journal of Sociology. 18*: 151–64.

SULLIVAN, H. S. 1953. *An interpersonal theory of psychiatry.* New York: W. W. Norton & Company, Inc.

SUSSMAN, M. B. and BURCHINAL, L. G. 1962. Kin family network: Unheralded structure in current conceptualizations of family functioning. *Marriage and Family Living. 24*: 231–40.

SUTTON-SMITH, B. and ROSENBERG, B. G. 1970. *The sibling.* New York: Holt, Rinehart, & Winston, Inc.

TURNER, R. H. 1964. *The social context of ambition.* San Francisco: Chandler Publishing Company.

United States Bureau of the Census, *Current Population Reports*, Series P-20.
   No. 148, School enrollment: October 1964. February 8, 1966.
   No. 168, Negro population: March 1966. December 22, 1967.
   No. 183, Characteristics of students and their colleges: October 1966. May 22, 1969.
   No. 185, Factors related to high school graduation and college attendance: 1967. July 11, 1969.
   No. 186, Marriage, fertility, and childspacing: June 1965. August 6, 1969.
   No. 194, Educational attainment: March 1969. February 19, 1970.
   No. 198, Marital status and family status: March 1969. March 25, 1970.
   No. 200, Household and family characteristics: March 1969, May 8, 1970.
   No. 204, Selected characteristics of persons and families: March 1970. July 13, 1970.
   No. 206, School enrollment: October 1969. October 5, 1970.

United States Bureau of the Census. 1960. *Persons by family characteristics.* Report PC(2)4B.

United States Commission on Civil Rights. 1967. *Racial isolation in the public schools.* Washington, D.C.: Government Printing Office.

United States Department of Labor, *Special Labor Force Reports.*
   No. 94, Marital and family characteristics of workers. March 1967, April 1968.
   No. 103, Educational attainment of workers. March 1968.
   No. 106, Job losers, leavers, and entrants. April 1969.
   No. 108, Employment of high school graduates and dropouts. October 1968.

No. 120, Marital and family characteristics of workers. March 1968 and 1969.

VIGOTSKY, L. S. 1962. *Thought and language.* Cambridge, Mass.: M.I.T. Press.

WALDMAN, E. 1970 Women at work: Changes in the labor force activity of women. *Monthly Labor Review,* June. Pp. 10–18.

WALLER, W. 1932. *The sociology of teaching.* New York: John Wiley & Sons, Inc.

WHITEMAN, M. and DEUTSCH, M. 1968. Social disadvantage as related to intellective and language development. In *Social Class, Race and Psychological Development,* ed. M. Deutsch, I. Katz, and A. R. Jensen. New York: Holt Rinehart & Winston, Inc.

WHORF, B. L. 1956. *Language, thought and reality.* Cambridge, Mass.: M.I.T. Press.

WILSON, A. B. 1969. Social class and equal educational opportunity. In Harvard Educational Review, *Equal Education Opportunity.* Cambridge, Mass.: Harvard University Press.

WINCH, R. F. 1962. *Identification and its familial determinants.* Indianapolis: The Bobbs-Merrill Co., Inc.

WYLIE, P. 1942. *Generation of vipers.* New York: Holt, Rinehart, & Winston, Inc.

WYLIE, R. C. 1961. *The self concept: A critical survey of pertinent research literature.* Lincoln, Nebr.: University of Nebraska Press.

SUBJECT INDEX

Academic performance: (*see also* Education; Schools; Teachers); class differences, 72-76, 97-100, 102, 121-25, 129-30, 144-45, 148; evaluation, 65, 67-69, 78, 143; failure, 96, 99, 101-2, 121, 143; and I.Q., 73-74, 85 n, 97, 97 n; and language, 72-74, 143; and parental involvement, 68-69, 74, 99; and peer influence, 75, 99, 103, 143; and racial differences, 143-46, 150, 151; and school characteristics, 99, 143, 145, 151; and personality, 74 n, 98-99, 101-2, 143, 145, 150-51; sex differences in, 75-76, 100-102, 106, 144; and values, 65-68, 71-72, 76-77, 97-99, 102, 116, 121

Adolescence: and adult society, 81-82, 86-88, 91-92, 94-97; decisions, 82, 93-97, 120-21; and identity, 81-83, 87-89, 90 n, 93, 100; and independence, 13, 81-82, 87, 90-92, 101-2; modeling, 86-89, 91-92; opportunity structure, 82, 94, 96-98, 102-3, 120-21, 127-28; parent-child relationship, 81, 90-94, 96; peer group values, 87-90, 93 n, 96-97, 102-3; sex-role socialization, 88-89, 92, 100, 102, 142

Blacks (*see* Negro)

Child rearing practices: class variations of, 41-44, 47-48, 54-59, 99, 117-18, 126-27; parent-child relationship, 41-51, 90-92; and class differences, 42-54, 57-58, 99, 117-18, 121-25, 134; and personality, 53-59, 64, 91, 99, 141-42, 150-51; and racial differences, 140-41

Class, social: (*see also* Mobility, social); academic performance of, 72-76, 97-100, 102, 121-25, 144-45, 148; aspirations of, 123-32; child rearing practices, 41-44, 47-48, 54-59, 99, 117-18, 126-27; as context for socialization, 126-36; education attained by, 5-6, 62-64, 78-79, 105-8, 121, 123-24, 145-46, 148-49; and family patterns, 110-16, 123-24, 139-41, 147-50; and I.Q., 151-52; language of, 49-51, 72-74, 121, 123-24, 142-43; and marital patterns, 113-17, 133-34, 140-44; occupational roles of, 5-6, 15, 44-46, 103, 108-10, 117, 123-24, 136, 139, 146, 148-49, 152; parent-child relationships in, 43-48, 54-55, 57-59, 98-99, 117, 121, 123-25, 134; peer group influence in, 70-72, 74-75, 88, 103, 123-24, 134, 142, 148; and personality, 46, 54-59, 66-69, 74 n, 98-99, 121, 123-24, 128, 130; and preparation for school, 66-72, 102, 117, 123-24, 126, 129-30, 132-34; and race, 38, 138-139, 143-152; sex differences in, 101-2, 106-8; socialization sequence of, 120-25, 127-33, 139, 148; values, 44-48, 58-59, 66-68, 71-72, 75, 98-99, 116-17, 121, 123-24, 134

Cognitive Development, 48-52, 57-58, 64

Dependency, 26-28, 36-37, 53

Education: (*see also* Academic performance; Schools; Teachers); and age at marriage, 110-11, 115-16, 121; as channel of mobility, 37, 102-3, 121, 148-49; and college attendance, 107-8, 113-14 n, 139, 146; as determinant of class position, 5-6, 36, 101-3, 121, 148-49; and equality of opportunity, 12-13, 35-36, 62-64, 78-79; and income, 109-10, 112-15; and marital relationships, 114-18, 140-41; and occupation, 5, 37, 44-45, 75, 78, 101, 108-10, 113-17, 146-49; and racial differences, 107 n, 139, 145-49; and sex differences, 106-8, 113-14 n, 145-46; and social class, 5, 62-64, 78-79, 105-8, 121-24, 143-46, 148-49; and unemployment, 109-10, 112-13, 115-16; and values, 65, 116-17, 134

164

139; and maturation, 80-81, 100-101; and peer group development, 70-71, 75, 142; and self-concept, 101, 140-42, 150-51

Significant others: (*see also* Family, nuclear; Peer group; Teachers); definition of, 18-19; and expectations, 126-32, 135-36, 148; and extra-familial contacts, 19-20, 27, 30, 32-33, 35-37, 60-62, 119-20, 126-27, 129, 143-45; and family, 18-20, 28-30, 36-37, 53-54, 66, 92-93, 119-20, 140-42, 150-51; and need gratification, 23, 26-35, 53; responses of, 126-30, 135, 148; in schools, 19-20, 28; and values, 27-29, 53, 119, 129-30

Socialization process: agents of, 1-4, 11-15, 18-20, 23-33, 35-37, 40-44, 50-51, 53-54, 57, 60-62, 64-65, 68-72, 74-78, 81, 83-84, 87-89, 94, 96, 99-102, 116, 119-21, 126-27, 132, 134, 140-41, 145, 150-51; class as basis for expectations, 126-33, 135-36; and class as context, 126-36; definitions, 1, 3-4, 17-18, 104, 116, 119-20, 126; diversity from, 2-3, 60-62, 77-78, 89, 99-100, 132-36, 138; interactive nature of, 103, 119-20, 126-33, 143, 148; and interpersonal influences, 18-37; as learning of roles, 31-32, 57-58, 104-5, 117; as link between origin and destination, 6-7, 15-17, 41, 102, 117-18, 127-29, 137; and opportunity structure, 56, 78-79, 82, 94, 96-97, 102-3, 120-21, 127-28, 132-33, 137-38, 148, 152; outcomes of, 17, 33-37, 52-54, 58, 64-66, 68-69, 76-78, 122-28, 148-52; and participation of socializee, 19-20, 23 n, 25-27, 29-37, 43, 52, 82-83, 92-93, 96-97, 119-21, 126-32; and social structure, 2-16, 120-21, 127-28, 132-33

Teachers: child's adjustment to, 66-67, 71, 75; and child's self-concept, 72, 74 n, 143; expectations, 66-68, 75, 100-101, 126-27, 134, 143; and language, 142-43; as models, 66 n, 86-87; and peer group influence, 71-72, 74-75, 77-78, 96-97; social class of, 66-67, 71, 78, 143; as socialization agents, 13, 19, 28, 36, 64, 67-68, 71-72, 74-77, 120, 127, 134, 143; values of, 84-86

Tuition, 20-21, 28-29, 34-36, 43, 46-47, 53-54, 67-68

Values: and academic performance, 64-65, 68, 71-72, 76-77, 97-99, 102, 116, 121; and achievement motivation, 45-46, 55, 98-99, 121, 142, 150; acquisition of, 29-30, 32-33, 52-53, 58, 76-77, 91-93, 99; and class differences, 44-46, 58-59, 66-68, 98-99, 116-17, 123-24; and occupation, 43-46, 56, 121, 134; and peer group, 35-36, 70-72, 75-77, 87-89, 93 n, 96-97, 102; of teachers, 84-86; and teacher's influence, 67-68, 71-72, 74-78

Women: (*see also* Sex differences); and child care, 19, 23-30, 37, 53-55, 66, 119, 142, 147; and dependence of status, 15, 38, 101, 110, 113-14 n; and dominance in family, 140-41, 147; and educational level, and age at birth of children, 111, 115, 121, 147; and educational level, and age at marriage, 110-11, 115, 121, 147; employment of, and children, 15 n, 110-14, 140; employment of, and income level, 112-16, 140; employment of, and racial differences, 140-41; as heads of households, 139-41; and marital role, 114-15, 140-41; and sex-role, 80-81, 89 n, 100-102, 113-15, 147; and sex-role socialization, 15, 38, 70-71, 87-89, 92, 100-101, 142

NAME INDEX